Salesforce Platform App Builder Certification

A Practical Study Guide

Rakesh Gupta

Apress®

Salesforce Platform App Builder Certification: A Practical Study Guide

Rakesh Gupta
Katihar, India

ISBN-13 (pbk): 978-1-4842-5478-3   ISBN-13 (electronic): 978-1-4842-5479-0
https://doi.org/10.1007/978-1-4842-5479-0

Managing Director, Apress Media LLC: Welmoed Spahr
Acquisitions Editor: Susan McDermott
Development Editor: Laura Berendson
Coordinating Editor: Rita Fernando

Cover designed by eStudioCalamar

Cover image designed by Pixabay

Distributed to the book trade worldwide by Springer Science+Business Media New York, 233 Spring Street, 6th Floor, New York, NY 10013. Phone 1-800-SPRINGER, fax (201) 348-4505, e-mail orders-ny@springer-sbm.com, or visit www.springeronline.com. Apress Media, LLC is a California LLC and the sole member (owner) is Springer Science + Business Media Finance Inc (SSBM Finance Inc). SSBM Finance Inc is a **Delaware** corporation.

For information on translations, please e-mail rights@apress.com, or visit http://www.apress.com/rights-permissions.

Apress titles may be purchased in bulk for academic, corporate, or promotional use. eBook versions and licenses are also available for most titles. For more information, reference our Print and eBook Bulk Sales web page at http://www.apress.com/bulk-sales.

Any source code or other supplementary material referenced by the author in this book is available to readers on GitHub via the book's product page, located at www.apress.com/9781484254783. For more detailed information, please visit http://www.apress.com/source-code.

Printed on acid-free paper

To Salesforce Ohana, which inspires, encourages, and supports me throughout my journey

Table of Contents

About the Author

Rakesh Gupta is a six-times Salesforce MVP, author, evangelist, Salesforce coach, and blogger, and is currently working as a Salesforce architect. He has authored six books on various Salesforce topics, and designed and delivered numerous Sales Cloud, Service Cloud, Community Cloud, Pardot, and Marketing Cloud solutions to a variety of organizations since 2011. He currently holds 15 certifications in Salesforce. He is best known as an automation champion in the Salesforce ecosystem, as he has written more than 200 articles on Lightning Flow and Process Builder to show how you can use Lightning Flow and Process Builder to minimize code use. Rakesh has trained more than 1000 individual professionals around the globe and has conducted several corporate trainings. He is the leader of the Navi Mumbai developer user groups in India and founder of the biweekly online webinar series Automation Hour. In addition, he is a well-known blog automation champion.
A graduate of SRM University, Chennai, India, with a major in IT, Rakesh now resides in Mumbai, India, and spends most of his free time writing blogs and books, and helping the Ohana Trailblazer community. He enjoys cooking, watching movies, and spending time with family and friends. You can follow him on Twitter (@rakeshistom) to get insights from his blog posts, and Salesforce tips and tricks.

About the Technical Reviewers

 **Philip Weinmeister**, Salesforce MVP, is the vice president of product management at 7Summits, where he focuses on building innovative components, apps, and bolts that enable impactful, transformative communities on the Salesforce platform. Phil is 20-times Salesforce certified and has delivered numerous Sales Cloud, Service Cloud, and (primarily) Community Cloud solutions to a variety of organizations on Salesforce since 2010. He released the first edition of *Practical Salesforce.com Development Without Code* in 2015 (Apress); in 2018, he released *Practical Guide to Salesforce Communities* (Apress). He has been a Salesforce MVP since 2015. He was named the first-ever Community Cloud MVP in 2017 and, in 2018, the Most Active Trailblazer by the Community Cloud team.

A graduate of Carnegie Mellon University with a double major in Business/IT and Spanish, Phil now resides in Powder Springs, GA. When he's not building solutions on Salesforce, he spends most of his "free" time with his amazing wife, Amy, and his children, Tariku, Sophie, Max, and Lyla. In addition to showing up at his kids' birthday parties as semisuperheroes, hoping for a winning season from the Arizona Cardinals, or rap battling his wife, he enjoys traveling, playing drums, and growing in his walk with Jesus. Stay updated on Phil's most recent insights and blog posts by following him on Twitter (@PhilWeinmeister).

Jitendra Zaa started his career as a J2ME developer in late 2006. He worked on many implementation projects in J2EE and ASP.Net technology until 2011. In 2008, he was introduced to Salesforce as part of a requirement to integrate Atlassian JIRA with force. com. Since then, he has worked on many Salesforce implementation projects as a technical architect, consultant, and lead developer. He has all Salesforce certifications except technical architect (pending Board review). In 2014, he was awarded Salesforce MVP by Salesforce.

Acknowledgments

First and foremost, I thank my parents, Kedar Nath Gupta and Madhuri Gupta; my sister, Sarika Gupta; and my brother-in law, Manish Kumar; for having patience with me for taking yet another challenge that decreased the amount of time I spent with them. They have been my inspiration and motivation for continuing to improve my knowledge, and the impetus to move my career forward. I thank Apress for giving me this opportunity to share my knowledge via this book. I also thank my friends Meenakshi Kalra and Munira Majmundar for helping me while I wrote this book.

A special thanks to all my well-wishers and friends. I especially thank reviewer Jitendra Zaa (Salesforce MVP) and Phil Weinmeister (Salesforce MVP). Without you, this book would never find its way to the Web. Last, I'm grateful to every member of Salesforce Ohana.

Introduction

Salesforce is currently one of the most demanding and fastest-growing enterprise software companies. *Salesforce Platform App Builder Certification: A Practical Study Guide* is a hands-on guide to help newbies (who have a basic knowledge of the Salesforce platform) or experienced Salesforce professionals who want to take their knowledge to the next level to become a Salesforce-certified platform app builder. As you read through this book, you will notice it focuses on real-world examples to help you acquire an understanding the Salesforce.com platform.

This book not only helps you clear Salesforce-certified platform app builder certification exams, but also exposes you to advanced Salesforce concepts such as platform security, customizing the Lightning interface, automation, social features, the application development life cycle, and more.

To get started, all you need is your brain, your computer with a modern web browser, and a free Salesforce developer org. You can sign up for a free developer org at `https://developer.salesforce.com/signup`. This is going to be an awesome experience, so let's get started!

I divided the book into eight chapters. The first chapter presents the fundamentals of the Salesforce platform. Chapter 2 exposes you to data models in Salesforce. In Chapter 3, we take a deep dive into Salesforce platform security. Chapter 4 gives you a ride on the Lightning Experience. In Chapter 5, we go through business process automation, followed by the Lightning Flow and Process Builder in Chapter 6. Chapter 7 deals mainly with the application development life cycle, whereas Chapter 8 focuses on Salesforce social features and analytics capabilities. Last, in each chapter, I provide a series of hands-on exercises designed to cement what you are learning in each chapter. I provide the answers to these exercises in the Appendix at the end of the book.

In *Salesforce Platform App Builder Certification*, I reflect thoughtfully on my years of experience working with the Salesforce platform and identify those areas that are most beneficial to you. I hope you find this book useful!

CHAPTER 1

Salesforce Platform Fundamentals

In this book, I take a hands-on approach to explain concepts you need to know to prepare for the Salesforce-certified platform app builder credential. New and intermediate developers need to have experience designing, building, and implementing custom applications using the declarative customization capabilities of the Salesforce platform, so let's get the ball rolling.

This chapter starts with an overview of the Salesforce platform followed by Sales and Service Cloud product offerings. We then take a close look at Lightning Experience and navigation items. In the second half of this chapter, we examine how AppExchange is changing the way customers use Salesforce. Last, we study the basics of the Salesforce platform.

Salesforce: A Brief History

In 1999, a few former Oracle executives (including Mark Benioff and Parker Harris) started Salesforce with a vision to provide cloud-based CRM systems to customers. CRM stands for *customer relationship management*. It allows companies to manage relationships with their customers and prospects, and also enables them to track all interactions, touch points, and so on. One can easily connect CRM with social media, phone, e-mail, and third-party channels to collect information about customers and prospects.

As it happens, a business may start with one vision in mind and, later, as it succeeds, it may add other products or services. For example, Apple Inc. started with one offering—computers—and later it added Macintosh, iPhone, iPad, and so on, to its offerings. The same business principle applied to Salesforce. As customers started to use

1

© Rakesh Gupta 2020
R. Gupta, *Salesforce Platform App Builder Certification*, https://doi.org/10.1007/978-1-4842-5479-0_1

its CRM system, the company expanded its offerings from Sales Cloud to include Service Cloud, Marketing Cloud, Integration Cloud, and more. In the past decade, Salesforce acquired more than 45 companies and expanded its cloud offerings. Now, Salesforce. com, Inc. has Sales, Service, Community, Marketing, Commerce, and Integration Clouds, as well as many other products. As a result, Salesforce in no longer *just* a CRM platform.

To give you an overview of how Salesforce has improved the user experience over time, Figure 1-1 shows what the Salesforce user interface looked like when I started my journey in 2011.

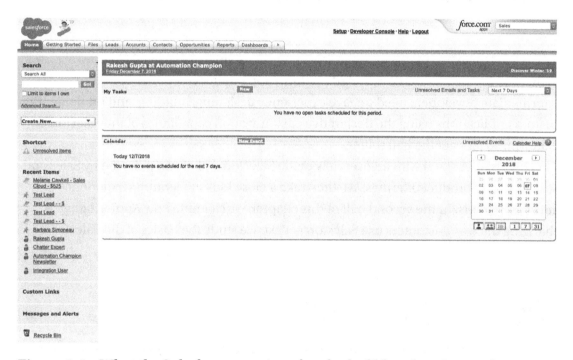

Figure 1-1. *What the Salesforces user interface looked like when I started my journey in 2011*

Figure 1-2 depicts what the user interface looks like now. What a difference eight years makes! Now Salesforce offers many ways to customize screens dynamically based on logged-in users. I talk about this more in upcoming Chapter 4.

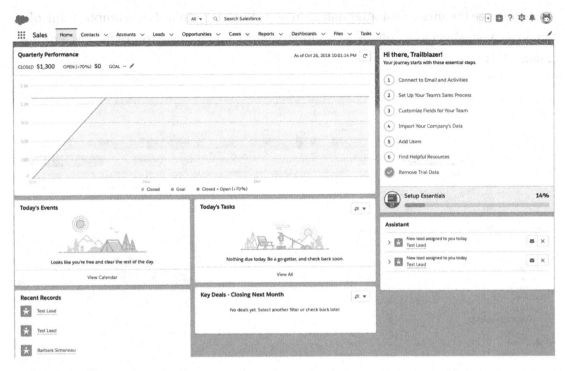

Figure 1-2. *What the Salesforce user interface (Lightning Experience) looks like today*

An Overview of the Salesforce Platform

Let's take a close look at how Salesforce stores data. Fundamentally, Salesforce uses spreadsheet concepts to organize data behind the scenes. It is similar to a database table. Salesforce fields are similar to database columns, and Salesforce records are similar to database rows (Figure 1-3).

First	Last Name	Company	Email
Rakesh	Gupta	Automation Champion	info@achamp.co
Susan	McDermott	Gurukul On Cloud	susan@gurukuloncloud.com

Figure 1-3. *The similarity between how Excel and Salesforce store data*

Salesforce organizes customer data into objects and records . For example, think of a tab on a spreadsheet as an *object*, a column as a *field*, and a single row of data as a *record* (Figure 1-4).

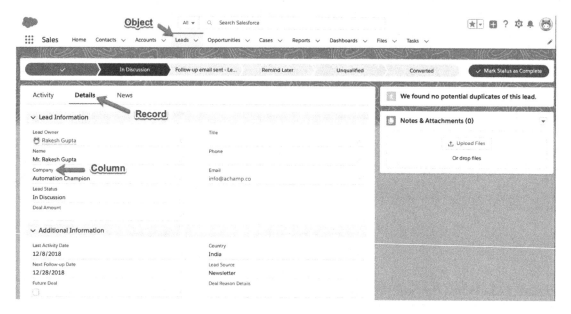

Figure 1-4. *Salesforce stores Excel spreadsheets, columns, and rows in its database*

Now pause for a minute and think. Do you understand what an object, a field, and a record are? If yes, then answer Hands-on Question 1.

HANDS-ON EXERCISE 1

Miranda Moonilal is working as a receptionist at GurukulonCloud (GoC). At GoC, they use a spreadsheet to store the details of a person's visit to its office. Miranda has a spreadsheet that contains 21 rows, including column names. The question for you is: if you upload the file to Salesforce, how many records will Salesforce create?

    a.   21

    b.   20

    c.   1

    d.   None

If your answer is correct, it means you have a solid, basic understanding of how Salesforce transposes spreadsheets to objects and records. To see the correct answer, go to the answer appendix at the end of this book.

Types of Objects in Salesforce

Objects are a key component in the Salesforce architecture. They provide the structure to store data and then display the data via the user interface to allow users to interact with the data. Salesforce provides the following types of objects:

- Standard objects
- Custom objects
- External objects

Standard Objects

After you set up a Salesforce org, you'll see that it comes with *standard objects*, which are provided as a core CRM structure. The objects include Lead, Account, Contact, Opportunity, Campaign, and more. They are the database tables that contain the records in any standard tab, such as Leads, Accounts, Contacts, Opportunities, Campaigns, and so on.

- **Lead**: A Lead object contains a prospect (not yet qualified) interested in your products or offerings.

- **Account**: An Account object stores data regarding the customers (and their company) with whom you're doing business.

- **Contact**: The Contact object includes people who work in your customers' company.

- **Opportunity**: The Opportunity object contains qualified leads. These leads are people who have talked to your sales team, expressed interest in continuing the conversation, and maybe even agreed to hear a sales pitch or look over a proposal. Opportunities are always associated with an account.

5

Custom Objects

In addition to standard objects, Salesforce allows you to create *custom objects* to store data specific to your organization. Because the data are specific to your organization, you may not be able to store org-specific data within the confines of a standard object. Custom objects are ideal for representing entities that are not represented appropriately by any standard object. An example is a custom object that stores employee time sheets, which doesn't come out of the box. Custom objects are usually identified by a __c suffix.

External Objects

External objects are similar to custom objects. They allow you to map the data stored outside of your Salesforce organization using Salesforce Connect. For example, you may have data stored in an enterprise resource planning (ERP) system. You can access these data, in real time, in Salesforce through external objects using Salesforce Connect. External objects are usually identified by a __x suffix.

Difference between Standard and Custom Objects

Let's take a look at the differences between standard and custom objects in Table 1-1.

Table 1-1. *Differences between Standard and Custom Objects*

Standard object	Custom object
Can't delete	Can delete
Can't change the Grant Access Using Hierarchies sharing access	Can change the Grant Access Using Hierarchies sharing access
Can't truncate standard objects	Can truncate custom objects

HANDS-ON EXERCISE 2

Pamela Kline is working as a system administrator at GoC. She needs some help identifying the custom object in the following options. Which answer will you give to Pamela?

a.   CampaignMember

b.   Leave_Balance__c

c.   Order__x

d.   Lead

To see the correct answer, go to the answer appendix at the end of this book.

Getting Started with Lightning Experience

Lightning Experience is a productive user interface designed to help sales teams close more deals faster and sell smarter. Lightning Experience is used to create a consistent user interface on all devices—from desktop to mobile. Lightning Experience, in a nutshell, is faster, better, and smarter.

A few years back, Salesforce announced Lightning Editions for Sales and Service Clouds. Lightning Editions is a completely reimagined packaging of Sales and Service Clouds. For a relatively small increase in price, Lightning Editions offers a host of additional functionality to customers, thereby increasing their productivity several-fold. Let's take a look at the following cloud editions:

- Sales Cloud Lightning Editions
- Service Cloud Lightning Editions

Sales Cloud Lightning Editions

Sales Cloud is a product designed to automate the sales process for an organization. By implementing Sales Cloud, an organization can boost its sales rep productivity. Sales Cloud includes core CRM object such as `Campaign`, `Lead`, `Account`, `Contact`, `Opportunity`, `Order`, `Report`, `Dashboard`, and so on. Salesforce offers various Sales Cloud editions to suit the business needs of varied organizations (Figure 1-5).

Figure 1-5. *Comparison of Sales Cloud Lightning editions*

- **Lightning Professional**: The Lightning Professional edition is
  designed for small- and medium-size businesses. It provides CRM
  functionality, including marketing, sales, and service automation. You
  can create a limited number of processes, role hierarchies, profiles,
  permission sets, and record types. For each Professional edition
  license, organizations currently have to pay US$75 per user per month.

- **Lightning Enterprise**: The Lightning Enterprise edition is designed for companies with complex business requirements. It includes all the features available in the Professional edition, plus it provides advanced customization capabilities through Apex programming and web service application programming interfaces (APIs) to integrate with third-party systems. For each Enterprise edition license, organizations have to pay US$150 per user per month.

- **Lightning Unlimited**: The Lightning Unlimited edition includes all Salesforce.com features for an entire company. It provides all the features of the Enterprise edition along with a new level of platform flexibility for managing and sharing all information on demand. The key features of the Lightning Unlimited edition are premier support, full mobile access, increased storage limits, and more. In addition, it also includes Work.com, Service Cloud, Knowledge Base, a live-chat feature, multiple sandboxes, and unlimited custom app development.

Note   When purchasing Salesforce.com licenses, organizations have to negotiate with a Salesforce account executive to get the maximum number of sandboxes. To know more about these license types, please visit the Salesforce web site at `https://www.salesforce.com/sales-cloud/pricing/`.

HANDS-ON EXERCISE 3

GoC has recently signed an agreement with a customer, Universal Containers (UC), to implement Salesforce Sales Cloud for them. UC wants to integrate Sales Cloud with their ERP system. At the minimum, which Sales cloud edition should UC purchase?

a. Lightning Unlimited

b. Lightning Professional

c. Lightning Enterprise

d. Lightning Essentials

To see the correct answer, go to the answer appendix at the end of this book.

Service Cloud Lightning Editions

Service Cloud is a product designed to streamline an organization's support process. By implementing this product, an organization can streamline support channels and consolidate all communication in Salesforce so support agents can channel their expertise in solving customer issues, rather than hunt for information (Figure 1-6). Salesforce provides various ways customers can connect with support agents, including live chat, computer telephony integration (CTI), video chat, social media, Salesforce Community, and so on.

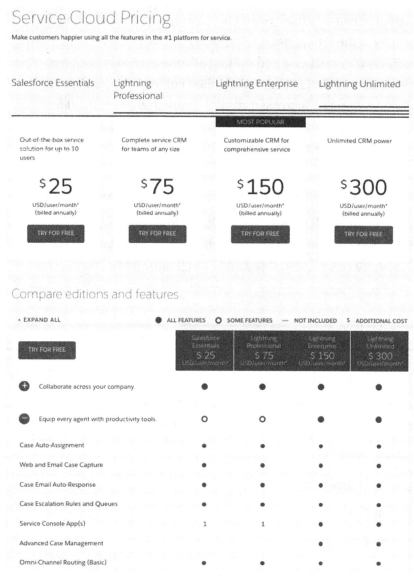

Figure 1-6. *Comparison of Service Cloud Lightning editions*

- **Lightning Professional**: The Lightning Professional edition is designed for small- and medium-size businesses. It includes features such as case management, CTI integration, mobile access, solution management, content library, reports, and analytics, along with sales features such as opportunity management and forecasting. You can create a limited number of processes, role hierarchies, profiles, permission sets, and record types. For each Professional edition license, organizations currently pay US$75 per user per month.

- **Lightning Enterprise**: The Lightning Enterprise edition is designed for companies with complex business requirements. It includes all the features available in the Professional edition, plus it provides advanced customization capabilities through Apex programming and web service APIs to integrate with other systems. It also includes Service Console, Service Contract, Knowledge Base, and Entitlement Management. For each Enterprise edition license, organizations currently pay US$150 per user per month.

- **Lightning Unlimited**: The Lightning Unlimited edition includes all Salesforce features for an entire enterprise. It provides all the features of the Enterprise edition and a new level of platform flexibility for managing and sharing all information on demand. The key features of the Lightning Unlimited edition include premier support, full mobile access, unlimited custom apps, increased storage limits, and more. It also includes Work.com, Service Cloud, Knowledge Base, live chat, multiple sandboxes, and unlimited custom app development.

Note   When purchasing licenses, organizations have to negotiate with a Salesforce account executive to get the maximum number of sandboxes. To learn more about these license types, visit the Salesforce web site at `https://www.salesforce.com/service-cloud/pricing/`.

Why Is Understanding Lightning Experience Important?

Lightning Experience is a new user interface that includes an artificial intelligence (AI) feature called Salesforce Einstein. It is easier to customize, faster to use, and smart enough to help you to close deals. Using Lightning Experience, you can enhance sales and support rep experience and productivity. You can create highly dynamic pages easily without writing a single line of code, which is quite cumbersome in Salesforce Classic, to say the least.

Salesforce Classic is the user interface customers were using before the launch of Lightning Experience. Although customers have the option to use Salesforce Classic, the transition to Lightning Experience has ushered in a new era for Salesforce by significantly transforming the way customers use Salesforce.

Sign up for Developer Playground

Salesforce offers free developer playground accounts to all administrators and developers. You can use the Salesforce playground to learn Salesforce by practicing new concepts and by building custom applications. Do not use Salesforce production/live instances to practice concepts. You can always use a Salesforce sandbox or free developer account (Figure 1-7) to practice the examples covered in this book. If you currently do not own a developer account, create a new one by visiting `http://developer.force.com/`.

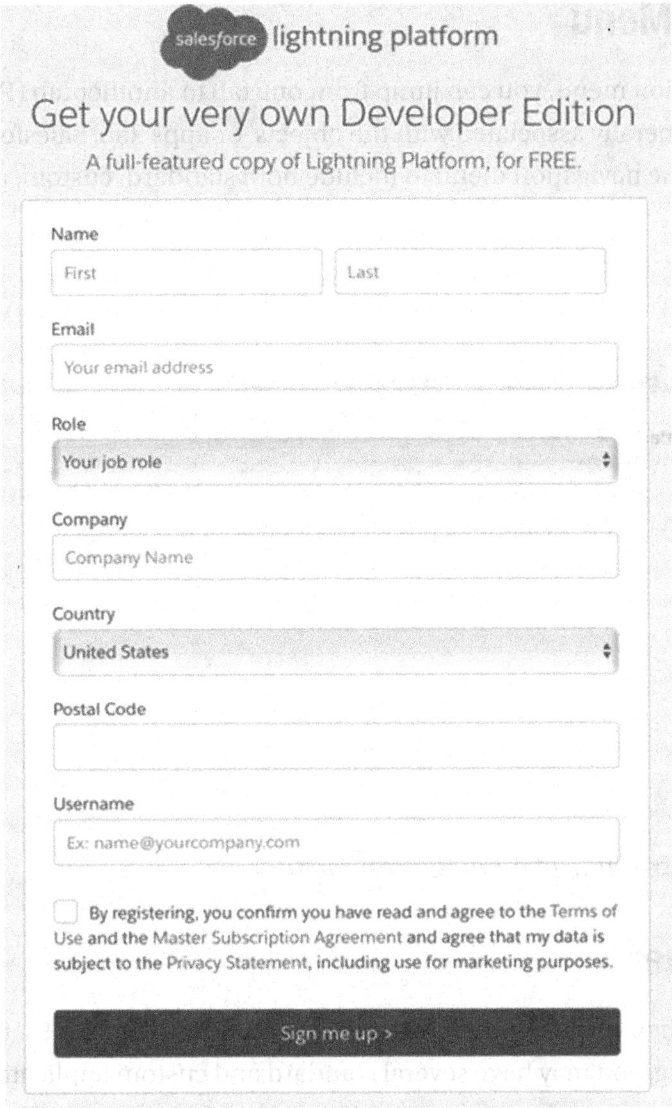

Figure 1-7. *Sign-up form for the Salesforce platform development environment*

After you register for a developer account, Salesforce.com, Inc. sends login details to the e-mail address you provide during registration. Follow the instructions in your e-mail to get started with Salesforce. After a successful login, you will be redirected to the Home tab (in the Lightning Experience user interface).

Navigation Menu

Using the navigation menu, you can jump from one tab to another tab (Figure 1-8). These tabs are generally associated with the objects' or apps' tab. Salesforce also allows us to customize the navigation menu to include both standard, custom, and external objects.

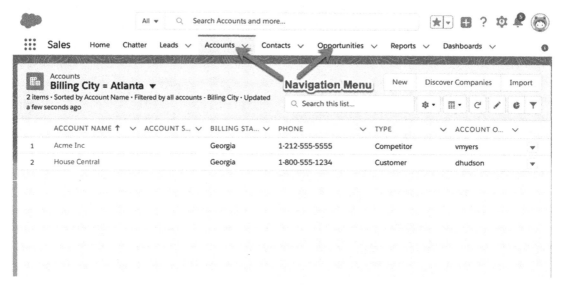

Figure 1-8. *An example of a navigation menu*

App Launcher

Using App Launcher, you can switch between applications (Figure 1-9). For example, in your Salesforce org, you may have several standard and custom applications. Currently you are in the Sales app and you want to switch to the Marketing app. You do this using App Launcher.

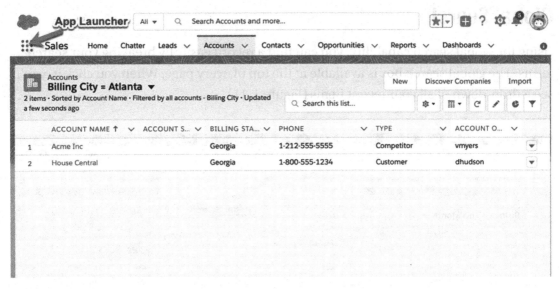

Figure 1-9. *An example of how to access App Launcher*

App Launcher provides a search feature to find apps by name. For example, if you want to find all apps that contain the letters "es," just type es into the search box, as shown in Figure 1-10.

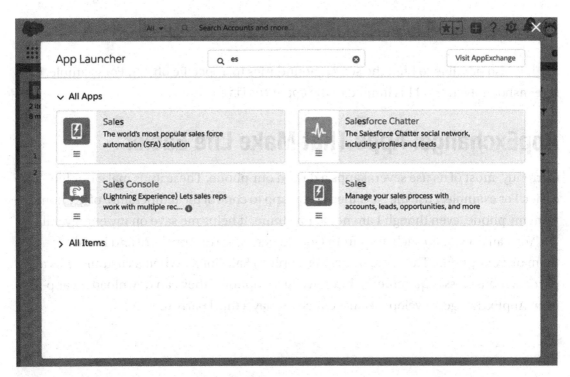

Figure 1-10. *App Launcher's search feature*

Global Search

Using the global search capability, you can find a record easily by breaking your search terms. The global search box is available at the top of every page. When you click it, you'll see a drop-down of all your recent items (Figure 1-11).

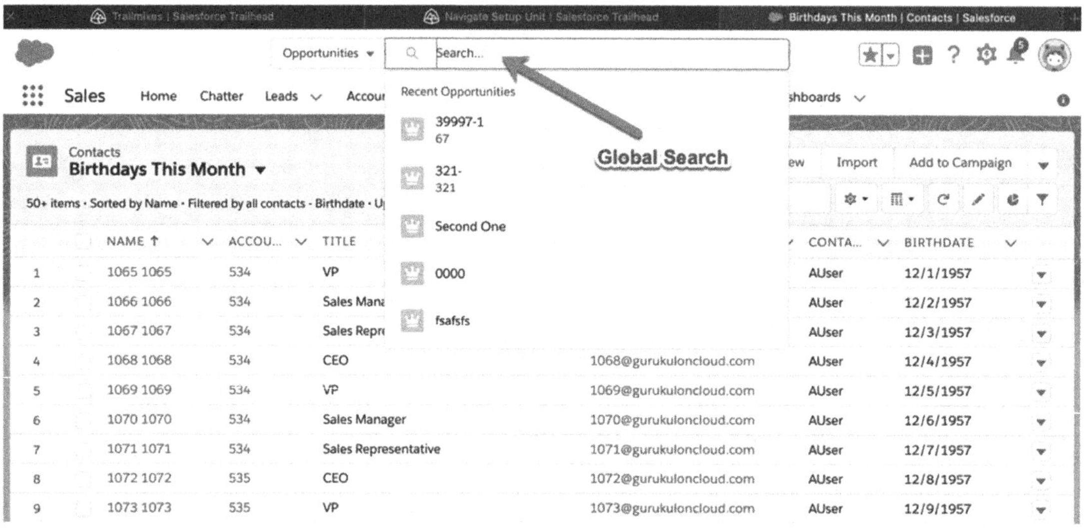

Figure 1-11. *An example of how to access the global search feature*

It is also possible to limit the search boundaries to a specific object. For example, the screenshot in Figure 1-11 is limited to the `Opportunities` object.

AppExchange: Apps That Make Life Easier

Currently, most of us use several apps a day on our phone. These apps make our life easier. For example, I use the Nest thermostat app to control the temperature of my home from my phone, even though I am not at my home. It helps me save on my energy bill.

You can download such apps from Google Play Store or App Store and install them on your phone. The same principles apply to Salesforce. When a customer has a particular business requirement, they have three options: they can download an app from AppExchange, develop it from scratch, or pay a third party to build it.

Let's look at the following business scenario: Robin Guzman just bought the Salesforce Lightning Enterprise edition. He has been working as a Salesforce administrator for few months when he receives the following requirements from his manager:

- Generate pdf documents using Account and Contact data

- Display all related contacts in the pdf

- E-mail the pdf to customers

Because Robin is an inexperienced Salesforce professional, he doesn't know how to provide the aforementioned requirements. So, he hops on the Salesforce Trailblazer Community (`https://success.salesforce.com/`) and posts his requirements there to get some help. Salesforce Trailblazer Community is a customer community managed by Salesforce.com, Inc. that allows customers to interact with other customers, partners, Salesforce enthusiasts, and product managers.

Someone from the community suggests Robin write code to provide the capabilities required. The problem is, Robin does not know how to write code in Salesforce. Another person suggests Robin use Conga Composer—an AppExchange app—to meet his requirements.

Robin is very excited about this advice and he navigates to the Salesforce AppExchange web site (`https://appexchange.salesforce.com`). At first, he is overwhelmed to see thousands of applications uploaded by partners, Interdependent software Vendor (ISVs), and consultants. He also learns that some apps are free whereas others must be purchased. Because Robin is looking for Conga, he types Conga in the search box and finds the application, as shown in Figure 1-12.

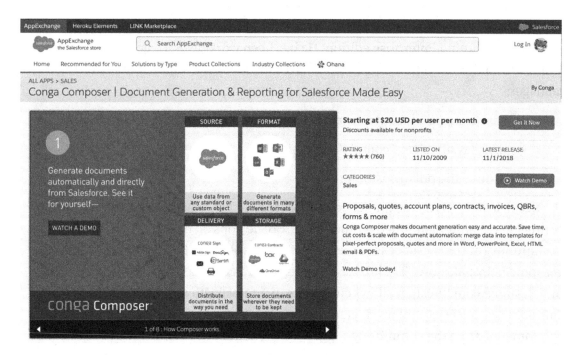

Figure 1-12. *An overview of the Conga Composer app in AppExchange*

Conga Composer allows Robin to generate documents automatically by using Salesforce data that he can then send to his customers.

Benefits of Using AppExchange Apps

There are certain benefits in using AppExchange over custom development:

1. **Development cost savings**: AppExchange apps save thousands of dollars that a company would have to spend to build a custom app.

2. **Quick deployment**: There is no need to wait for weeks until developers deploy a custom application. It is very easy to configure AppExchange apps. You can start using an app from AppExchange within a few hours of downloading it in your instance.

3. **Secure**: AppExchange apps are not only fast to install, but also all code are tested and passed by Salesforce itself, so customers can be assured that all apps go through a rigorous security review process.

4. **Upgradable**: Usually, paid apps are automatically upgraded when vendors release an enhancement.

5. **Well documented**: AppExchange apps are well documented, which may not be the case if you develop a custom app.

The Force.com Multitenant Architecture

Salesforce is built on top of Lightning Platform. Lightning Platform is a cloud-based platform used to develop enterprise applications. As a developer, you don't have to worry about network, hardware, platform maintenance, or downtime.

You may have heard that Salesforce is a multitenant architecture and wonder: *what is a multitenant architecture?*

In a multitenant architecture, a single system serves as a base service to all customers. This means system resources are shared among all customers (Figure 1-13).

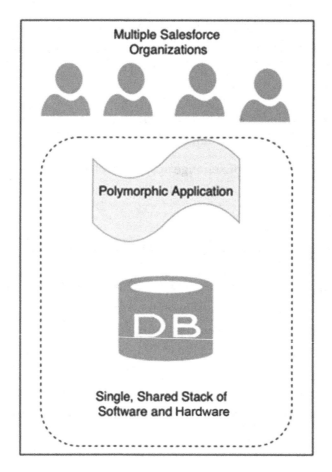

Figure 1-13. *Multitenant architectures control how resources are shared among customers*

Let's take a real-world example. If you live in a multistory building, you have your own space (say, a two-bedroom apartment). Other people live in the same building too. As a result, there is a common space everyone has to share.

The same concept applies to Salesforce. Salesforce provides a single copy of an app to all organizations that runs on the same Salesforce server. Customers are allowed to customize an org according to their business needs. Because several customers share the same Salesforce server, some limits are applied by Salesforce to make sure no one uses more resources than their allotted share. In formal terms, this is called a *governance limit*. Governance limits make sure an organization does not hit a threshold that might negatively affect the performance of the system as a whole, thereby affecting not only the organization that hit the threshold, but also all other "tenants" as well.

Additional Hands-on Exercises

The following exercises will give you more practice using Lightning Platform. Because these are straightforward exercises, no "answers" are included in the Appendix.

1. Explore Lightning Experience and find the Setup section.

2. Create one Lead, one Account, and one Contact record.

3. Switch to the Service app using AppLauncher.

4. Find all records with name *Acme*.

5. Update your profile image in Salesforce.

6. Log out of Salesforce.

7. Explore the Conga Composer app and find the reviews posted by other customers.

8. Install the Conga Composer app in your free developer account for admin only.

9. Navigate to the Conga Composer app in Salesforce.

Summary

In this chapter, we studied the Salesforce platform, including how Salesforce stores data in objects and fields. We also examined various Salesforce editions available on the market for sales and service clouds. Furthermore, we looked at a high-level overview of Lightning Experience. Last, we examined the advantages of AppExchange over custom development and we learned about Force.com architectures.

CHAPTER 2

The Underpinnings of Data Modeling

In the previous chapter, we looked at the Salesforce platform, including various Salesforce editions available on the market for Sales and Service Clouds. Furthermore, we took a high-level look at Lightning Experience. Last, we discussed the advantages of AppExchange over custom development and we studied the Force.com architecture.

This chapter is comprised of two parts. Part one is divided into three sections. In the first section, we review metadata and Schema Builder. In the second section, we examine different types of relationships possible in Salesforce. In the third section of part one, to deepen our understanding of the concepts discussed in the first and second sections, we explore a few real-world examples. Part two is divided in two sections. In the first section, we look at different field types and key considerations to make before changing field types. In the second section of part two, we study a use case of external objects.

Metadata: The Core of the Salesforce Platform

How is Salesforce able to deliver the best customer experience? What enables the Salesforce platform to be highly customizable? How is Salesforce able to separate customer data, customer customization (for example, list views, reports, and fields), and platform architecture? As we saw in Chapter 1, a multitenant architecture is a software architecture module in which multiple instances of software run on a single physical server. The server then serves multiple tenants. Apart from the Salesforce multitenant architecture, what else holds the key?

© Rakesh Gupta 2020
R. Gupta, *Salesforce Platform App Builder Certification*, https://doi.org/10.1007/978-1-4842-5479-0_2

Look No Further Than Metadata: It's the Key!

Metadata? What is that? I was stumped. I started researching and was awed by it! I spent hours peeling away the layers to achieve mastery over the concept, for it is, indeed, the key to understanding how Salesforce is able to deliver the best customer experience!

In a nutshell, metadata is information about data! Wait a minute! What? Yes, it is that simple. And yet, it is a complicated concept. So, let me take a crack at explaining it by providing three examples involving Pamela Kline, a Salesforce administrator at GoC:

1. On December 17, Pamela traveled from San Francisco to the Dallas–Fort Worth (DFW) Airport. At the airport, she met Julie Ball. Julie works at UC as vice president (VP) of sales. Julie likes to travel and she loves to explore new cities.

2. On December 24, Pamela met Jessica Murphy at Costco. Jessica is working at Northern Trail Outfitters as a store manager. Jessica likes to learn about new technology.

3. On December 26, Pamela met Jana Mickel, chief executive officer (CEO) of Acme Nonprofit, at Starbucks. Jana likes to inspire people by doing charity work on weekends.

Comb through the three previous scenarios carefully! When you do, one thing should stand out: the structural information in all three examples is the same, but the descriptive information is different. Let's create a table (Table 2-1) to visualize the concept.

Table 2-1. *How to Store Metadata in a Table Format*

Name	Place They Meet	Date They Meet	Company	Position	Interest
Julie Ball	DFW Airport	17 December	Universal Containers	VP of Sales	Travel
Jessica Murphy	Costco	24 December	Northern Trail Outfitters	Store manager	New technology
Jana Mickel	Starbucks	26 December	Acme Nonprofit	CEO	Charity work

Table 2-1 is just a table *until you realize it is comprised of metadata and data*. Metadata are column labels—in this case, Name, Place They Meet, Date They Meet, Company, Position, and Interest. The data, however, are Julie Ball, DFW Airport, December 17, UC, VP of Sales, travel, and so on. In other words, data are information *within* a column that is *different in each row*.

Let's look at another example to acquire an understanding of the difference between metadata and data:

- Metadata about music CDs are genre, composer, location of recording, record label, and so on.

- Metadata about books include subject, author, publisher, language, and year of publication.

- Metadata about photographs include photographer name, the date a photo was taken, subject, and location.

The Question Is: Why Do We Need Metadata?

Metadata help us find things. They are used to organize data! Let's look at an example to understand how metadata actually helps in real-life situations.

In a bookstore, one can find books by author (Figure 2-1).

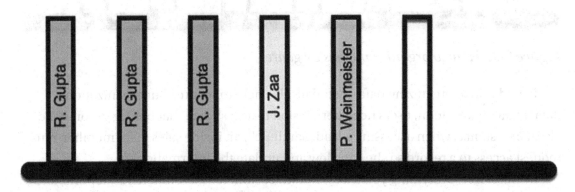

Figure 2-1. *How to organize books in a bookstore*

In a music store, one can find music CDs by artist name (Figure 2-2).

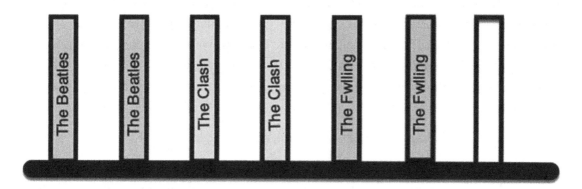

Figure 2-2. *How to organize CDs in a music store*

When renting a film, one can find movies by genre (Figure 2-3).

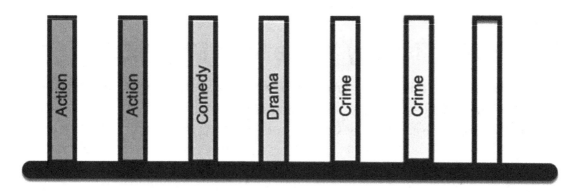

Figure 2-3. *How to organize movies by genre*

In addition to organizing data, metadata also help to secure your organization's data. In an organization, users need permission to access data that belong to someone else. For instance, when accessing a lead, Sarah Bell, an inside sales team member, must request access to a record so she can view and update the information.

In Salesforce, everything you access—from custom tabs, custom fields, reports, and so on—are metadata. They are the backbone of your Salesforce instance, with all your custom and standard functionality. Salesforce uses special metadata layers to separate customer customizations so that, despite upgrading the platform three times a year, it does not modify customer data or customizations inadvertently.

Understanding the Power of Schema Builder

Schema Builder is a tool that can be used to visualize and edit a data model. The tool comes in handy when you want to understand and design data models that are highly customized and complex.

Schema Builder is an interactive drag-and-drop tool that can be used to perform the following actions:

- View relationships between objects

- View the following objects on the canvas:

    - Standard objects

    - Custom objects

    - System objects, including `User`, `Task`, `Event`, and `Activity`

- Create and delete custom objects

- Modify properties of custom objects

- Create and delete custom fields

- Modify properties of custom fields

- Manage fields permission

Understanding the Data Model

As mentioned, Schema Builder can be used to understand the relationship between objects, or you can simply explore only one object by adding it to the canvas. Let's look at Schema Builder via a business use case.

Robin Guzman just bought the Salesforce Lightning Enterprise edition. He has been working as a Salesforce administrator for few months. Recently, he got an assignment to implement campaign management, and he wants to understand the relationships between the objects used in campaign management (`Lead`, `Contact`, `Campaign`, and `Campaign Members`).

Robin performs the following steps to meet the requirement with which he is tasked:

1.   He clicks Setup (gear icon) ➤ Setup Home ➤ Data ➤ Objects and Fields ➤ Schema Builder and then navigates to the Objects tab.

2.   Robin then selects the objects—Lead, Contact, Campaign, and Campaign Member—to display on the canvas (Figure 2-4).

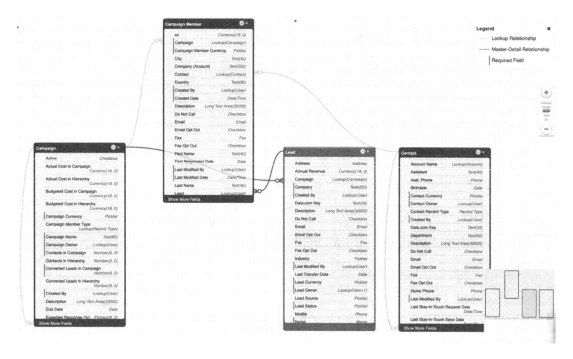

Figure 2-4.   *Selecting objects to display*

By looking at the screenshot in Figure 2-4, Robin understands *how these objects are connected.* He realizes that Campaign Member is the *junction object* that *connects* Lead and Contact to the Campaign object.

Creating a Custom Field

Custom fields are unique to your business needs. Creating custom fields allow you to store information that is unique to your organization. These fields can be added, amended, and deleted. Custom fields are usually identified by a __c suffix.

Back to Robin and our business scenario. Robin now understands how objects within a campaign connect to each other. He is thrilled by the power of Schema Builder. Having mastered the concepts behind it, Robin is ready to tackle the following new requirements:

- Add a custom field to the Lead object to store a credit score.

- Set the field length to 1 and the decimal places to 0.

Robin uses Schema Builder to fulfill these requirements as follows:

1. He clicks Setup (gear icon) ➤ Setup Home ➤ Data ➤ Objects and Fields ➤ Schema Builder and then navigates to the Objects tab.

2. Robin then selects Lead to display on the canvas.

3. Then he clicks the Elements tab.

4. Next, Robin selects the Number field and drags and drops it onto an object on the canvas. This action opens a window, where he enters the following details:

   a. **Field Label**: The label for custom field; in this case, he enters Credit Score as the label

   b. **Field Name**: The name of the field, which autopopulates based on the label

   c. **Description**: Meaningful text so another developer or administrator can understand easily why this custom field was created

   d. **Help Text**: Meaningful help text so whenever users hover over this field, they can understand easily what they have to enter in this field

   e. **Default Value**: A value for this custom field that is inserted automatically when a new record is created

   f. **Length**: The field length; in this case, Robin enters 1

g. **Decimal Places**: The number of digits to display after the decimal point; in this case, he enters 0

h. **Required**: An option for making a field required. In our case, Robin knows the best practice is to use a validation rule to make a field required; therefore, he does not select this check box.

i. **Unique**: An option for making a field unique. In our case, Robin does not need it to be a unique field, so he does not select the check box.

j. **External ID**: An option for making this field a unique record identifier from an external system

The result of these actions is shown in Figure 2-5.

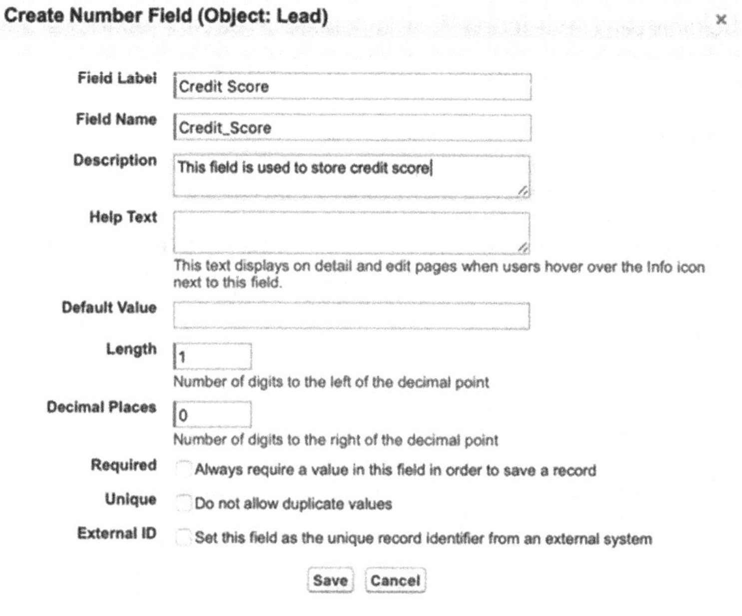

Create Number Field (Object: Lead)

Field Label	Credit Score
Field Name	Credit_Score
Description	This field is used to store credit score
Help Text	

This text displays on detail and edit pages when users hover over the Info icon next to this field.

| Default Value | |
| Length | 1 |

Number of digits to the left of the decimal point

| Decimal Places | 0 |

Number of digits to the right of the decimal point

Required	Always require a value in this field in order to save a record
Unique	Do not allow duplicate values
External ID	Set this field as the unique record identifier from an external system

Save   Cancel

Figure 2-5. *Screen to create a custom field using Schema Builder*

5. Last, Robin clicks the Save button.

Best Practice Tip   Instead of creating new custom fields, standard fields can be used by renaming the label.

Managing Field-level Security

It is a myth that Schema Builder can't be used to set field-level security. Let's set field-level security using Schema Builder and put the myth to rest once and for all using our business scenario.

Robin is very happy. He added his first field using Schema Builder. Now he must tackle another requirement: grant the `Credit Score` field Read/Write access to the following profiles:

- System administrator

- API user (custom profile)

Robin performs the following steps to provide the new business requirements using Schema Builder:

1. Right-clicks the `Credit Score` custom field.

2. Selects `Manage Field Permissions`, as shown Figure 2-6.

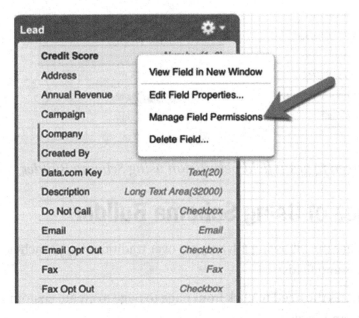

Figure 2-6. *Screen to manage field permission using Schema Builder*

3. These actions open a window that Robin uses to set up field-level security based on the stipulated requirements. He grants access to System Administrator and API User only (Figure 2-7), then clicks the Save button.

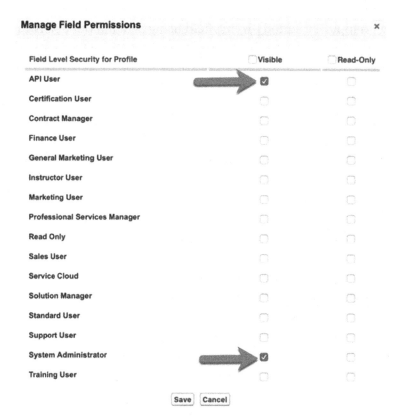

Figure 2-7. *Screen to grant field permission using Schema Builder*

Advantages of Using Schema Builder

Schema Builder has the following advantages over traditional approaches to create, edit, and delete objects and fields:

- Eliminates the need to click from page to page to create custom objects and fields.

- Is a graphical way to analyze relationships between objects.

- Adds fields and objects without leaving Schema Builder.

- Saves time when creating multiple fields.

Understanding Relationship Types in Salesforce

When you create a relationship between two objects, you select a relationship type to determine how closely associated you want the related records to be. You can connect a standard object to another standard or custom object and vice versa. For example, if you have a custom object named Event (where you store information about upcoming events) and you want to associate it with another custom object, Registrant (to store information about registrants for a particular event), you can associate the registrant records with the respective event record.

These relationship types also control how *record sharing*, *data deletion*, and *required fields* in the page layout are handled. The following are the types of relationships that can be established between objects:

- Lookup relationship

- Self-relationship

- Master detail relationship

- External lookup relationship

- Indirect lookup relationship

- Many-to-many relationship (junction object)

- Hierarchical relationship

Lookup Relationship

Lookup is a loosely connected relationship among Salesforce objects. It means if someone deletes the parent record, the child records remain in the system. In a lookup relationship, both parent and child have separate shared settings (Figure 2-8).

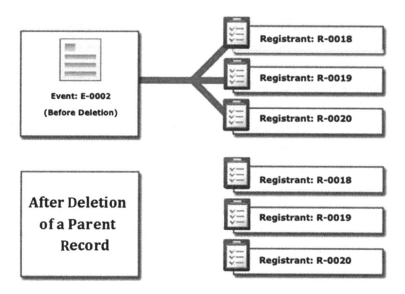

Figure 2-8. *An example of a lookup relationship*

For example, suppose there is a lookup relationship between the Event custom object and the Registrant custom object in which Event acts as the parent object and Registrant is a child object. If someone deletes the Event record, all related Registrant records remain in the system without the parent (Figure 2-9).

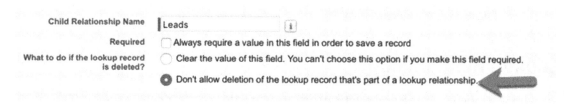

Figure 2-9. *Settings available for a lookup relationship*

Please study Figure 2-9 carefully. When you do, you should notice that if you select the check box Don't allow deletion of the lookup record that's part of a lookup relationship, then it is not possible to delete a parent record that has child records! However, in such a scenario, *you could delete the child record without any issue*!

Self-relationship

Self-relationship is a type of lookup relationship. You can use the lookup relationship to create a self-relationship between objects. You can have a maximum of 40 lookup relationships in an object. For example, a Case record can have a Parent Case record, as shown in Figure 2-10.

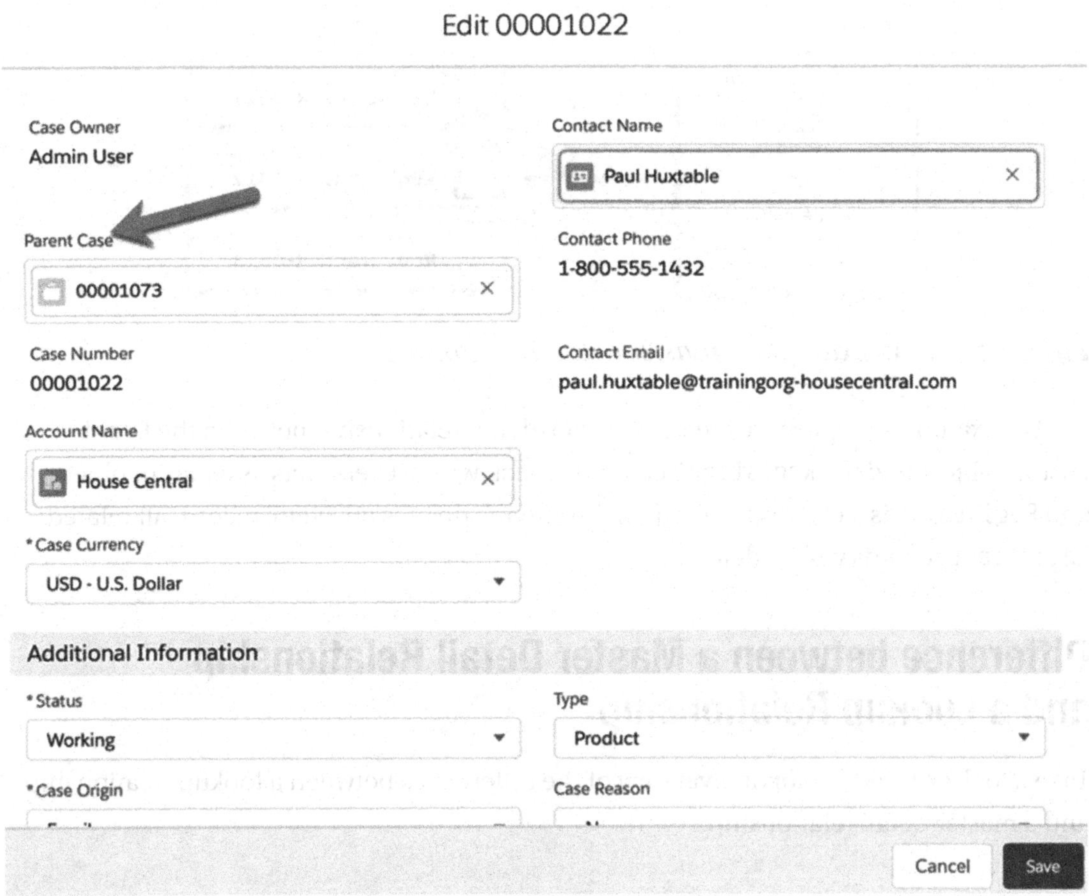

Figure 2-10. *An example of a self-relationship*

Master Detail Relationship

Master detail is a strongly connected relationship between Salesforce objects. It means that if someone deletes the parent record, the child records are also deleted. In this type of relationship, the parent record controls the accessibility of its child records. It also means that if users have access to a parent record, they also have access to the related child records (Figure 2-11).

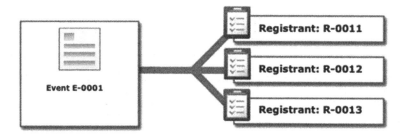

Figure 2-11. *An example of master detail relationship*

For example, suppose we create a master-detail relationship between the Event custom object and the Registrant custom object, where Event acts as a parent object and Registrant is a child object. Then, if someone deletes an Event record, all related Registrant records will be deleted.

Difference between a Master Detail Relationship and a Lookup Relationship

Take a look at Table 2-2 for an overview of the differences between a lookup relationship and a master detail relationship.

Table 2-2. *Difference between Lookup and Master Detail Relationships*

Lookup Relationship	Master Detail Relationship
Are loosely connected.	Are strongly connected.
Rollup summary field cannot be created.	Rollup summary field can be created.
Parent record is not required (it's optional) when creating a child record.	Parent record is always required to create a child record.
Lookup fields are not required on the page layout of the detail record.	The `Master Detail` field is always required on the page layout of the detail record.
A standard object record can be on the detail side of a custom object record.	A standard object record cannot be a child or on the detail side of the relationship.
Record ownership of child records is not controlled by the parent.	The parent controls record ownership of child records. The `Owner` field is not available in the child record in a master detail relationship.
You can have a child record without a parent.	You cannot have a child record without a parent.
You can have maximum of 40 lookup relationships on an object.	You can have maximum of two master detail relationships on an object.

External Lookup Relationship

When you create an external object in Salesforce, you are introduced to two new lookup relationships: an external lookup relationship and indirect lookup relationship. An external lookup relationship allows you to establish a relationship between a child standard, custom, or external object and an external parent object with data stored in an external data source.

Indirect Lookup Relationship

An indirect lookup relationship allows you to establish a relationship between a child external object and a parent standard or custom object. You can only create an indirect lookup to an object that has a unique external ID field on the parent object that is used to match the records in this relationship. When creating an indirect lookup relationship field on an external object, you have to specify the child object field and the parent object field to match and associate records in the relationship. For example, you can display a related list of payments from the Systems Applications Products (SAP) external record by matching external IDs on the `Account` object.

Many-to-Many Relationship

The many-to-many relationship in Salesforce allows you to associate a child record with multiple parents, and vice versa, with the help of an intermediate object. For example, a campaign is attached to multiple leads and one lead may be associated with more than one campaign.

If you want to relate two objects—for example, `Account` and `Contact`—in such a manner that one account can have multiple contacts associated with it, you have to use a many-to-many relationship. To establish a many-to-many relationship, you have to use a third object known as a *junction object* (Figure 2-12). Indeed, to establish a many-to-many relationship between `Account` and `Contact` objects, Salesforce offers a junction object known as `AccountContactRelation`.

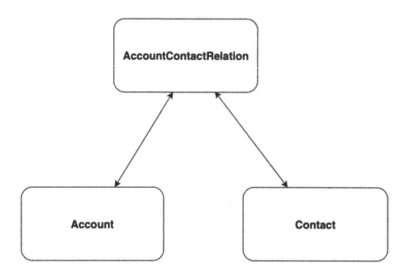

Figure 2-12. *An example of a many-to-many relationship*

Hierarchal Relationship

A hierarchical relationship is only available in the `User` object. With this type of relationship, you can create a hierarchy of users in an organization. For example, a user can have a reporting manager (custom hierarchical field, as shown in Figure 2-13) and her reporting manager may have another reporting manager and so on until the CEO level.

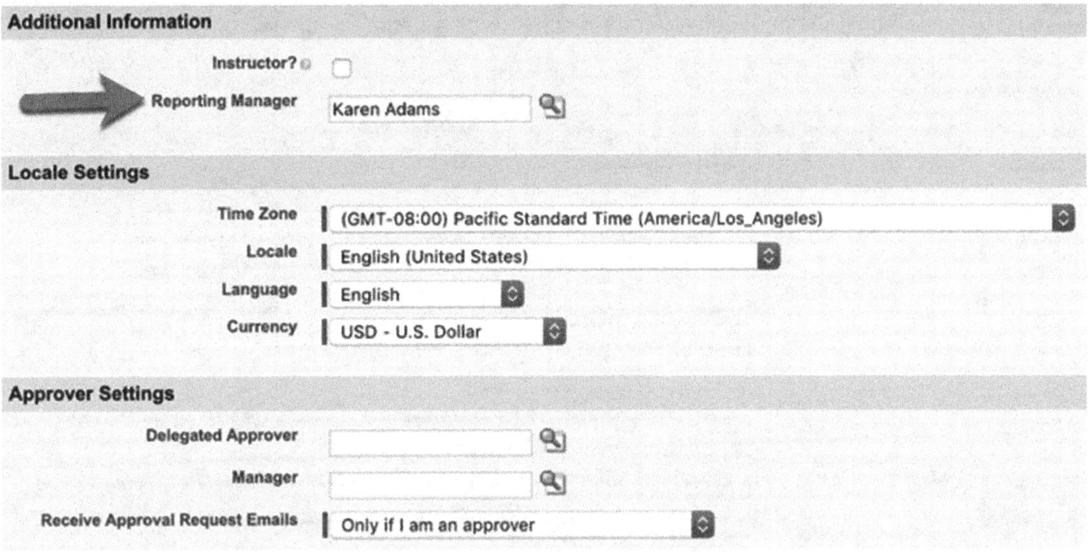

Figure 2-13. *An example of a hierarchical relationship*

Selecting the Appropriate Field Type

When we studied Schema Builder, we created a field. Now let's take this topic further and look at how one selects a field type.

As we now know, all objects in Salesforce have a predefined set of fields to store common business information, known as *standard fields.* It is possible to customize the standard field's label and help text; however, you cannot delete or rename the API of a standard field.

Sometimes, it is necessary to create a custom field instead of using a standard field. For example, to store a Social Security number, you need to display the last four digits to an end user like XXX-XX-1234. To achieve this, you create a custom field. Salesforce allows you to add custom fields to standard and custom objects to capture additional information required for your business. The best part is, if you create a custom field and then later find you no longer need it, you can delete it.

When creating a custom field, the first step is to select the field type, such as Email, Text, Number, Geolocation, and so on. These field types come with system-defined validation rules (Figure 2-14).

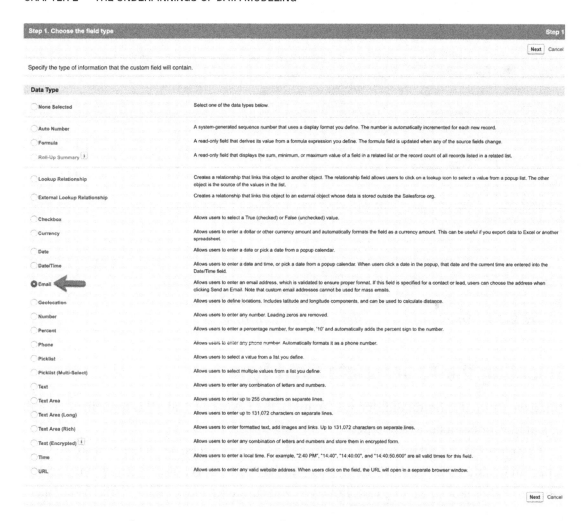

Figure 2-14. *Selecting an appropriate field type*

For example, if you select Email as the field type, users are allowed to enter an e-mail address that is validated, by the system, to ensure the proper format is used. There are some field types that allow you to maintain data quality, such as Picklist, Picklist (Multi-Select), and Checkbox.

HANDS-ON EXERCISE

- Explore how many different field types are available when creating a custom field.

- Write down the properties of the `Picklist`, `Checkbox`, and `Text` (`Encrypted`) field types and notice the differences.

Because this is a straightforward exercise, an "answer" is not provided in the Appendix.

Understanding Field Dependencies

To maintain data quality, Salesforce allows you to establish field dependencies between fields. Field dependency means the control value of one field is based on the value of another field. For example, if users decide to receive a newsletter, you can ask them to select the type of newsletter they would like to receive, as shown in Figure 2-15.

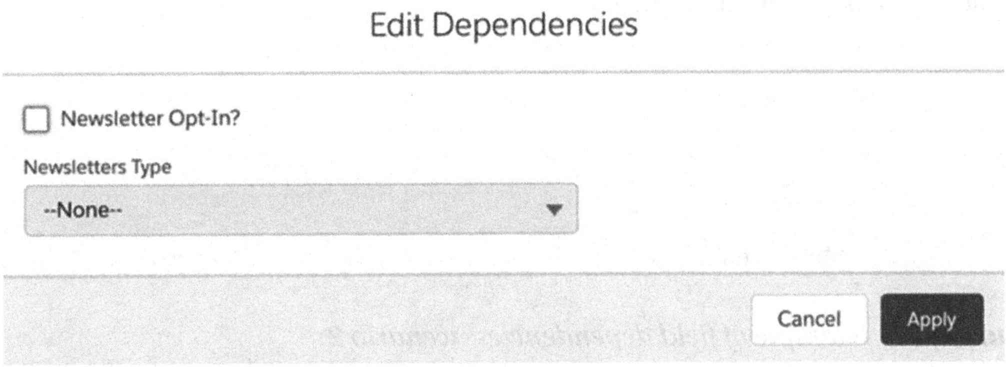

Figure 2-15. *How field dependencies can be used*

When you look at Figure 2-15 carefully, you might notice that the `Newsletters Type` field is Read Only because the `Newsletter Opt-In?` field is not yet selected.

Now let's select the `Newsletter Opt-In?` field and then select a newsletter type, as shown in Figure 2-16.

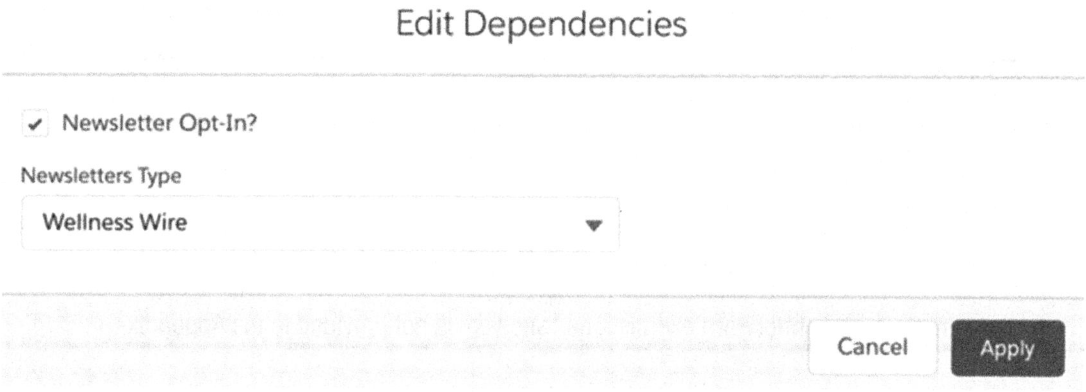

Edit Dependencies

✔ Newsletter Opt-In?

Newsletters Type

Wellness Wire ▼

Cancel   Apply

Figure 2-16. *Example of field dependencies: scenario 1*

Let's take another scenario. If field dependencies are not in place, then users are able to select a newsletter type without opting-in to receive a newsletter (Figure 2-17). This not only doesn't make any sense, but also such inconsistencies in the data impact data quality negatively. It is important to understand the role of field dependencies and how they affect data quality and integrity. As a best practice, whenever possible, use field dependencies to improve data quality.

Newsletter Opt-In?

Newsletters Type

Men's Health ▼

Figure 2-17. *Example of field dependencies: scenario 2*

HANDS-ON EXERCISE

- Create one check box field on the Lead object Newsletter Opt-In?

- Create one more field (Newsletters Type) on the Lead object. The data type of the field should be Picklist with the following values:

  - Wellness Wire

  - Nutrition

  - Women's Wellness

  - Men's Health

  - Becoming a Mother

  - Senior Health

  - Allergies

  - Bipolar Illness

  - Breast Cancer

Because this is a straightforward exercise, an "answer" is not provided in the Appendix.

Setting up Field Dependencies

Now that we've studied field dependencies, it's time to set them up. Let's go back to our business scenario. Robin Guzman wants to understand the process of establishing field dependencies between the Newsletter Opt-In? and Newsletters Type fields. He performs the following steps:

1. He clicks Setup (gear icon) ➤ Setup Home ➤ Object Manager ➤ Lead ➤ Fields & Relationships.

2. He selects the Field Dependencies button, which redirects him to the field dependencies management page.

3. Robin navigates to the field dependencies-related list and clicks the New button, as shown in Figure 2-18.

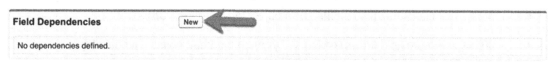

Lead Field Dependencies

Help for this Page 🔲

This page allows you to define dependencies between fields (e.g., dependent picklists).

Field Dependencies   New   ⬅

No dependencies defined.

Figure 2-18. *First screen of the field dependencies setup process*

> 4. He selects Controlling Field and Dependent Field, as show in
>   Figure 2-19.

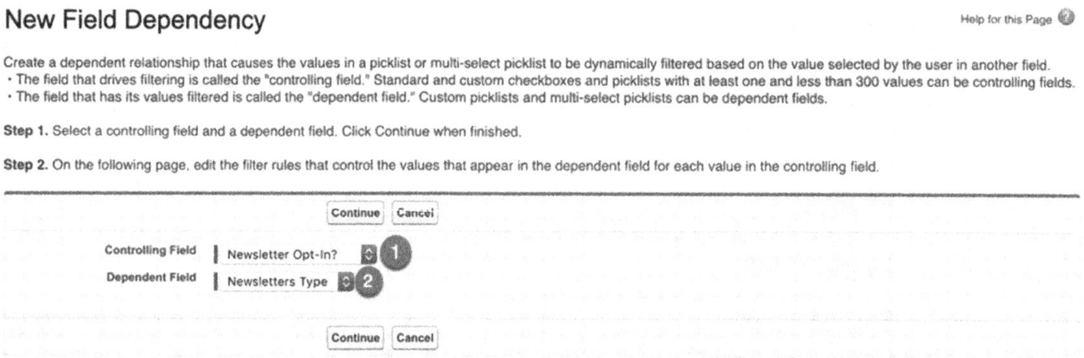

New Field Dependency

Help for this Page 🔲

Create a dependent relationship that causes the values in a picklist or multi-select picklist to be dynamically filtered based on the value selected by the user in another field.
• The field that drives filtering is called the "controlling field." Standard and custom checkboxes and picklists with at least one and less than 300 values can be controlling fields.
• The field that has its values filtered is called the "dependent field." Custom picklists and multi-select picklists can be dependent fields.

Step 1. Select a controlling field and a dependent field. Click Continue when finished.

Step 2. On the following page, edit the filter rules that control the values that appear in the dependent field for each value in the controlling field.

Continue Cancel

Controlling Field | Newsletter Opt-In? ⬍ ①
Dependent Field | Newsletters Type ⬍ ②

Continue Cancel

Figure 2-19. *The second screen of the field dependencies wizard allows the administrator to select Controlling Field and Dependent Field*

> 5. Robin then clicks the Continue button.
>
> 6. He selects the appropriate newsletter types in each column by
>   double-clicking them (Figure 2-20).

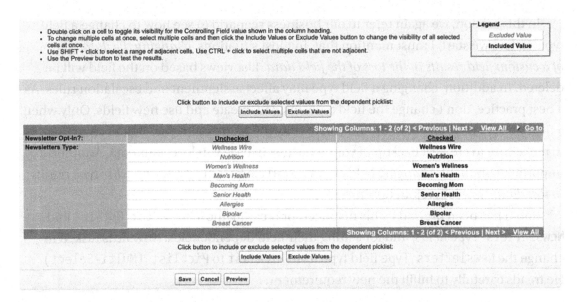

Figure 2-20. *The third screen of the field dependencies wizard allows the administrator to select values for the dependent picklist*

7.   Last, he clicks the Save button.

Tip   Check out the help documentation published by Salesforce to learn more about dependent fields (https://help.salesforce.com/ articleView?id=fields_dependent_field_considerations. htm&type=5).

Implications of Changing a Field's Type

By now, you should be clear on what a field type is, how field dependencies affect data quality, and how to set up field dependencies. If there is *any* confusion about these topics, reread the material and master the concepts. When you master them, you will almost be ready for your Platform App Builder exam!

Note   Review Salesforce release notes to ensure you are abreast of the latest developments on the platform.

In this section, we again refer to our business scenario to see how to change a field type. Before we start, I must mention that, in most situations, *changing the data type of a custom field results in the loss of the field data.* List views based on the field will be deleted. In addition, changing a field type may affect assignment and escalation rules. As a best practice, don't change the field type; instead, create and use new fields. Only when a field doesn't have any data should you modify the field's data type. Before changing it, make sure to create a backup of your data, just in case you lose your data. Another important comment: *changing to* Picklist (Multi-Select) *from any other type results in lost data.* Now let's rejoin Robin.

Robin has been praised by his manager for creating the Newsletter Opt-In? and Newsletters Type fields, and for setting their field dependencies. Now he is tasked to change the Newsletters Type field type from Picklist to Picklist (Multi-Select). He treads carefully to fulfill the new requirement:

1.   Robin clicks Setup (gear icon) ➤ Setup Home ➤ Object Manager ➤ Lead ➤ Fields & Relationships.

2.   Next he clicks the Edit link available next to the Newsletters Type custom field, as shown in Figure 2-21.

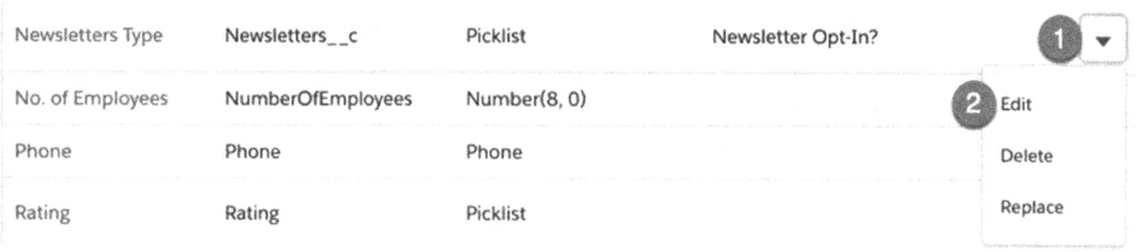

Figure 2-21.   How to edit a field from the object manager

3.   Then he clicks the Change Field Type button, as shown in Figure 2-22.

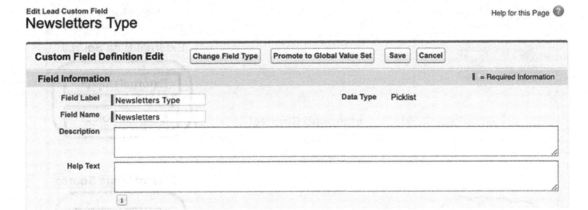

Figure 2-22. How to change the field type for a custom field

4. He selects the new data type: `Picklist (Multi-Select)`.

5. Then he clicks the `Next` button.

6. At this point, Robin can change the field label, name, and any other attributes.

7. Last, he clicks the `Save` button.

Tip   Check out the help documentation published by Salesforce to learn more about changing custom field types (`https://help.salesforce.com/articleView?id=notes_on_changing_custom_field_types.htm&type=5`).

Exploring External Objects

An external object is similar to a custom object. External objects are usually identified by a __x suffix. They allow you to bring data from external systems (data stored outside your Salesforce organization) to your Salesforce org without writing any code. Figure 2-23 depicts the process using Lightning Connect.

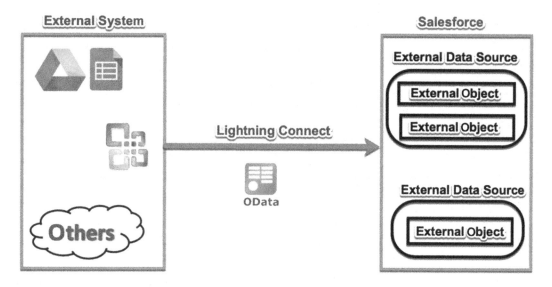

Figure 2-23. *How an external system and Salesforce are connected via Lightning Connect*

Each external object relies on an external data source definition, such as Lightning Connect or OData, to connect with an external system. You can connect each data table from an external system to an external object. Each of the external object fields maps to a table column in the external system.

Tip To get hands-on experience using external objects, I highly recommend exploring this Trailhead module: `https://trailhead.salesforce.com/en/ content/learn/modules/lightning_connect/lightning_connect_ integrate`.

Points to Remember

- Schema Builder can't be used to export the org schema.

- The `Geolocation` field is not available through Schema Builder.

- Not all standard objects are available in Schema Builder. For example, `AccountShare` and `OpportunityContactRole` are not visible.

- It is a best practice not to create more than 10,000 child records in a master detail relationship.

- In the case of lookup relationships, if you delete a parent and also want to delete related child records, reach out to Salesforce support to enable such feature.

- When you enable reporting on a custom object, Salesforce creates a new report type to build reports on it.

- When you create relationships with other objects, Salesforce creates additional report types so you can include related records in the same report.

- You can define a custom `Picklist` field as a `Controlling` or a `Dependent` field.

- The standard `Picklist` field must be a `Controlling` field; it can never be a `Dependent` field.

- It is not possible to change field types for standard fields.

- It is not possible to select `Picklist (Multi-Select)` as a `Controlling` field.

- It is not possible to select `Checkbox` as a `Dependent` field.

- It is not possible to change the data type of a standard field.

- One Salesforce org can have 100 external objects. External objects do not count against the number of custom object limits.

Hands-on Exercises

The following exercises give you more practice with the platform, which ultimately helps you gain mastery of the platform and helps you prepare for the certification examination. Remember, these are hands-on exercises and you can find the answers in the Appendix at back of the book, but try to implement the exercises in your Salesforce org.

1. Use Schema Builder to learn about the data model of the following objects:

   a. `Product`, `Price Book`, and `Price Book Entry`

   b. `Opportunity` and `Opportunity Product`

   c. `Quote` and `Quote Line Item`

2. Add the custom field `Next Meeting Date` to the `Opportunity` object using Schema Builder to store the next meeting date. Set the field-level security (Read/Write) for the following standard profiles:

   a. System administrator

   b. Contract manager

   c. Marketing user

3. Dennis Williams is a system administrator at GoC. He is tasked with creating a field to store Social Security numbers. He also needs to mask all the characters so no one can see the data behind the field. Which field types should he use?

4. Dennis is required to create one field in the `Contact` object to store client photographs. Which field type should he use?

5. Dennis is tasked with creating a field that allows users to store customer geolocation, including latitude and longitude. Which field type should he use?

6. Denise wants to implement opportunity management at GoC, but he is a bit confused by one of the requirements. Because you now have a better understanding of field types, please help him select the appropriate field type to display the `Account Site` field value in the Opportunity record.

   In addition, Dennis needs the `Account Site` field to show the latest value. This means that if the value of the `Account Site` field is changed from Mumbai to Dallas, then the `Account Site` field value should reflect Dallas.

7. Create two custom picklist fields per the following requirements:

    a. Country (Picklist Multi-Select): India, United States, Japan, China, Canada, The Netherlands, United Kingdom, Spain, Mexico, Brazil, Peru, Colombia, and Greece. Sort these values in alphabetical order.

    b. Business Region (Picklist): APAC, EMEA, NA, and LATAM. Sort these values in alphabetical order.

    c. Set up field dependencies between the Business Region and Country fields based on the following table:

Business Region	Country
APAC	India, Japan, China
EMEA	Spain, The Netherlands, Greece, United Kingdom
NA	United States, Canada
LATAM	Mexico, Brazil, Peru, Colombia

8. Help Dennis select the appropriate relationship field to connect the Consumer (parent) and License (child) custom objects. Later, he plans to create a rollup summary field on the parent object.

9. Dennis has been given the task of establishing a relationship between the Meetup__c and Participants__c objects. He needs to achieve the following capabilities:

    a. If users delete the Meetup record, they will get an error message if there are child Participant records associated with it.

    b. Dennis needs to make sure the parent lookup field is marked "required" on the child record. Which field type should he use?

10. Create two custom objects: Meetup and Participants. Here are the fields for both objects:

    a. Meetup object: Meetup Start Date/Time, Meetup End Date/Time, Location Details, Description, and Meetup Name. Meetup Name should be an autonumbered field.

b. Participants object: `First Name`, `Last Name`, `E-mail`, `Date of Birth`, `Phone`, `Mailing Address`, `Annual Income`, and values for status drop-down are Yes and No.

Now establish a lookup relationship between these two objects. Insert a few Participant records without associating them with a Meetup record. Change the relationship type from lookup to master detail.

11. Keeping the previous exercise in mind, create a field in the Meetup record to the show number of people who answered yes while RSVPing.

Summary

In this chapter, we examined the basics of metadata and why we need it, followed by an in-depth look at Schema Builder. We also studied various relationship types available in Salesforce. Furthermore, we looked at field types, field dependencies, and implications of changing field types. Last, we examined external objects and their use cases. In the next chapter, we take an in-depth look at platform security and settings.

CHAPTER 3

Platform Security

In Chapter 2, we examined Salesforce data modeling, metadata, and Schema Builder. Furthermore, we studied the different types of relationships possible in Salesforce. Last, using real-world examples, we saw how to select field types for a field and studied the implications of changing a field type.

This chapter is comprised of two parts. First, we cover

- Organization-wide default (OWD)

- Role hierarchies

- Record sharing

- Profiles

- Permission Set

- Custom permission

In the second part of this chapter, we look at how to set up security at the object and field levels.

OWD: A Baseline Setting for Objects

As noted in the previous list, OWD stands for organization-wide default. When I started learning Salesforce in 2012, the following questions haunted me:

1. What is OWD?

2. How does OWD affect Salesforce record accessibility?

3. Who can set up OWD?

4. What are the key considerations for setting up OWD?

53

© Rakesh Gupta 2020
R. Gupta, *Salesforce Platform App Builder Certification*, https://doi.org/10.1007/978-1-4842-5479-0_3

By the end of this section, you'll know the answers to these questions. We explore each question in detail, so let's get started.

Have you ever wondered the following?

- Why is it that I am able to view and/or edit records owned by some users but not by others?

- Why is it that I am not able to view and/or edit records that are not owned by me?

- Why is it that I am not able to view and/or edit the records that are owned by me!?

Look no further than your organization's OWD settings! Let us decrypt OWD and get to the bottom of this.

OWD is a security design model. It is a baseline setting for objects in a Salesforce org that determines default record access for all users, and for all records, within each object!

It is one of the simplest, *and* one of the most complicated, concepts. Yes, an oxymoron indeed! So, let us explore it through examples of Pamela Kline, a Salesforce administrator at GoC:

1. Pamela resides at 1622 Davidson Street, Alpharetta. No outsiders—except her friends and family—are allowed on the premises. This means it is *private* property. Another example is an office space. If an office space is marked *private*, people entering the space without permission could be punished or even jailed for trespassing. A Private model enables owners of the property to prohibit access to outsiders.

2. On December 24, Pamela went to IKEA to buy a new couch. There, she met Julia Roberts, a sales manager. Julia helped Pamela find the perfect couch. IKEA is a *public* place, so Pamela could go and access the entire store, *but she is not allowed to change any settings in the store.* Another good example is a museum. People can visit, explore, and learn at museums, but they cannot dictate where a painting or an artifact can be placed. These examples are equivalent to a Public Read-Only model in Salesforce, in which users can view a record owned by others, but they do not have permission to make any changes to the record.

3. Pamela is keen to learn new stuff on the Internet. Munira Majmundar, Pamela's neighbor, introduces her to Wikipedia. Wikipedia is a free online encyclopedia created and managed by volunteers across the globe. Anyone can update a Wikipedia page if they find something inaccurate. This is equivalent to a Public Read/Write model in Salesforce.

When you comb through these examples carefully, one thing should stand out: *the permission level, in each of the three scenarios, is different*—namely, Private, Public Read Only, and Public Read/Write. See Table 3-1 to visualize the concept.

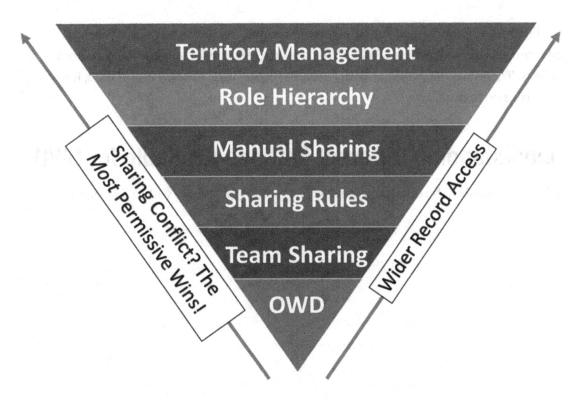

Figure 3-1. *Controlling data access with the Salesforce platform*

Table 3-1 is just a table until you realize that it comprises of real-life examples mirroring Salesforce's OWD terminology!

Table 3-1. *Representation of Real-life Examples with Respect to Salesforce OWD*

Places	Permission Levels	Actions One Can Perform	Salesforce-equivalent OWD
Pamela's house	Private property	None (except for Pamela and her friends and family)	Private
IKEA	Open to public, with read permission	View	Public Read Only
Wikipedia	Open to public, with modified permission	View/edit	Public Read/Write

Figure 3-1 demonstrates major pillars that control record-level sharing among different sets of users, where OWD is the base-level setting for standard and custom objects. Therefore, one cannot restrict a user's record-level access below OWD. It is the most restrictive of all.

Understanding Different Settings Available for OWD

Table 3-2 describes the different types of OWD settings available within Salesforce.

Table 3-2. *Different Types of Salesforce OWD Settings*

OWD Settings	Explanation
Private	When OWD of an object is set to Private, the record is visible to the owner. Create-Read-Update-Delete (CRUD) access is required to perform CRUD actions, which we discuss later in this chapter.
	If owners are assigned a role and the `Grant Access Using Hierarchies` check box is checked, then the owners have complete access (read, edit, delete, and share) to records they own and all the records owned by users below in the role hierarchy. Note: *The Grant Access Using Hierarchies feature is checked by default on standard objects and cannot be unchecked.*
Public Read Only	When OWD of an object is set to Public Read Only, it allows users to view all records of an object. CRUD access is required to perform CRUD actions.
	If owners are assigned a role and the `Grant Access Using Hierarchies` check box is checked, then the owners have complete access (read, edit, delete, and share) to records they own and all the records owned by users below in the role hierarchy.
	This permission allows users to report on records to which they have access.
Public Read/Write	When OWD of an object is set to Public Read/Write, users can view and edit all records of an object. CRUD access is required to perform CRUD actions.
	In this case, if the `Grant Access Using Hierarchies` check box is checked, then all users have complete access (read, edit, and delete) to records they own and all the records owned by users below them in the role hierarchy.
	This permission allows users to report on all records.
Controlled by Parent	This option is used if you want to allow users to view the related (child) records only when they have access to the parent record. CRUD access is required to perform CRUD actions.

(continued)

Table 3-2. (*continued*)

OWD Settings	Explanation
Public Read/Write/ Transfer	This option is used if you want to allow users to view, edit, and transfer all records. This setting is only available for `Case` and `Lead` objects.
	This permission allows users to report on all records.
Public Full Access	This option is used if you want to allow users to view, edit, delete, and transfer all records. This setting is only available for the `Campaign` object.
	This permission allows users to report on all records.
Use (available for price book)	This option is used if you want to allow users to view the price book and associated products. This setting allows them to use the price book on an opportunity.
View Only (available for price book)	This option is used if you want to allow users to view the price book and associated products, but don't want to give them the ability to use the price book on an opportunity.
No Access (available for price book)	With this option, users with Manage Price Book permission can access price books for maintenance.

Predefined OWD for Objects

When you create a new Salesforce org, it comes with OWD settings for standard and custom objects. Salesforce gives you the ability to modify them per your business needs. You can view your org's default OWD settings by navigating as follows: Setup (gear icon) ➤ Setup ➤ SETTINGS ➤ Security ➤ Sharing Settings. The predefined OWD access for standard and custom objects is shown in Table 3-3.

Table 3-3. *Predefined OWD Access for Standard and Custom Objects*

Object	Default Access
Account	Public Read/Write
Activity	Private
Asset	Controlled by Parent
Campaign	Public Full Access
Campaign Member	Controlled by Parent
Case	Public Read/Write Transfer
Contact	Controlled by Parent
Contract	Public Read/Write
Custom object	Public Read/Write
Lead	Public Read/Write Transfer
Opportunity	Public Read Only
Order	Controlled by Parent
Price Book	Use
Users	Public Read Only, and Private for external users

Importance of Role Hierarchy

Role hierarchy has a major impact on record sharing in Salesforce. Therefore, defining the hierarchy correctly for your org is a critical design consideration.

The role hierarchy may or may not mirror your company's hierarchy. Depending on your business needs, you can create users with or without assigning them a role. Similarly, a role can have one or more than one users assigned to it.

The role hierarchy works in conjunction with OWD. When studying various OWD settings, you may have noticed that, if an owner has a role and the Grant Access Using Hierarchies check box is checked, then users have complete access (read, edit, delete, and share) to records they own and to the records owned by users below them in the role hierarchy. Remember: OWD determines access to objects, but it is the role hierarchy that grants users access to records they own and records owned by users below them in the role hierarchy.

Use Case 1

Pamela Kline is working as a system administrator at GoC. She is currently implementing campaign management. She understands how objects within a campaign connect with each other. Pamela is given the following requirements:

- Inside sales team members should not able to view leads owned by other inside sales team members.

- The inside sales manager, however, should be able to view, edit, and share access to leads with any users assigned to inside sales team members.

Figure 3-2 shows GoC's current organizational chart.

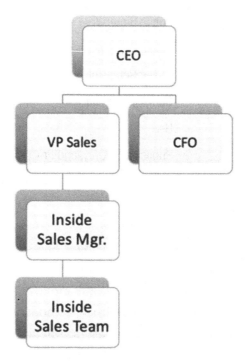

Figure 3-2. *An abbreviated functional organizational structure of GoC*

Before developing any solution, think OWD, because it is the *base-level setting* that restricts object-level access in Salesforce. For Pamela to meet her requirements, she has to set OWD for the Lead object to Private and Grant Access Using Hierarchies to True.

Pamela performs the following steps to meet the requirements using OWD:

1. She clicks Setup (gear icon) ➤ Setup ➤ SETTINGS > Security ➤ Sharing Settings ➤ Edit.

2. Pamela navigates to the OWD settings for the Lead object and sets Default Internal Access to Private.

3. If you look at Figure 3-3 carefully, the Grant Access Using Hierarchies field is *selected by default* and users are not allowed to change this setting. However, on custom objects, you have the option of selecting this option. By granting access, the inside sales manager can access Lead records assigned to the inside sales team.

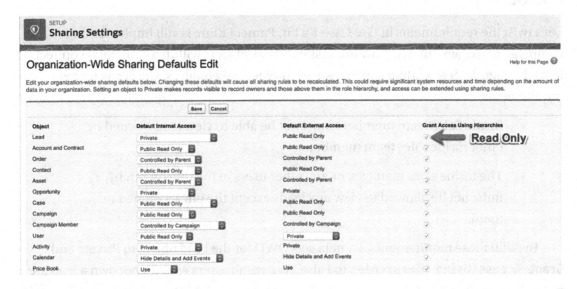

Figure 3-3. *OWD settings*

4. When done, Pamela clicks the Save button.

Table 3-4 explains internal and external access for organization-wide settings.

Table 3-4. *Difference between Internal and External Access*

Access	Explanation
Default internal access	Internal access is for internal user license types.
Default external access	External users include the following licenses: • Guest users • Chatter external users • Community users • Customer portal users • High-volume portal users • Partner portal users • Service Cloud portal users • Authenticated web site users

Use Case 2

Let's twist the requirements in Use Case 1 a bit. Pamela Kline is still implementing campaign management. She now understands how objects within a campaign connect to each other. After attending a meeting with project stakeholders, she is given new requirements:

- Inside Sales team members must not be able to view leads owned by other inside sales team members.

- The inside sales manager, or any other users in the role hierarchy, must not be allowed to view any leads except the ones assigned to them.

To fulfill these requirements, Pamela sets OWD for the Lead object to Private and Grant Access Using Hierarchies to False. As a result, users who do not own a lead are not able to see it.

Oh! You caught the Herculean error in Pamela's solution, right? You realized that Pamela *cannot set* Grant Access Using Hierarchies to *False* for the Lead object because the Lead object is a standard object, and therefore Grant Access Using Hierarchies is checked *by default and users are not allowed to change it.* Bravo!

Because it is not possible to change `Grant Access Using Hierarchies` on a standard object, as you correctly noted, Pamela has to create a workaround. As a result, Pamela toys with the following possible options:

1. Create a custom object to store leads—for example, `Prospect__c`.

    a. Set custom object `Prospect__c` OWD to Private.

    b. Set `Grant Access Using Hierarchies` to False.

2. Use a standard `Lead` object.

    a. Set `Lead` object OWD to Private.

    b. Set `Grant Access Using Hierarchies` to True (because you can't change it).

    c. Use Visualforce Page or Lightning Web Component as a main interface.

    d. Behind the scenes, write custom logic to display the record based on the owner!

These possible workarounds demonstrate how a single setting in Salesforce—in this case, `Grant Access Using Hierarchies`—can pose challenges if you fail to understand their implications.

Setting up Role Hierarchies

Whenever users are created, as a best practice, the system administrator should always assign a role to them. If no role is assigned, users are only able to view/access records assigned to them, assuming OWD is set to Private. Note that users can only be assigned a role at the system level, not the object level.

Please make sure you read and reread the previous section on the importance of role hierarchies so you thoroughly understand the significance a role plays in Salesforce with regard to enabling users to access and share records they own or do not own.

It is worth repeating: *only* if users are assigned a role can the system administrator grant them read, edit, delete, and share access to records owned by them or owned by users below them in the role hierarchy. For instance, even if two users are at the same level—such as the chief operating officer (COO) and the chief information officer (CIO)—they are not able to access each other's records until they have a role assigned to them, assuming that OWD for the object is not Public Read Only or Public Read/Write.

Recall that the role hierarchy works in conjunction with OWD—meaning, whether the role hierarchy affects access to a record depends on the OWD value set for the object. If OWD for an object is Public Read Only, then every user in the organization would be able to view the records within the object. Simple—assuming they have read access via profiles.

Take a minute to review GoC's organizational chart as shown in Figure 3-4.

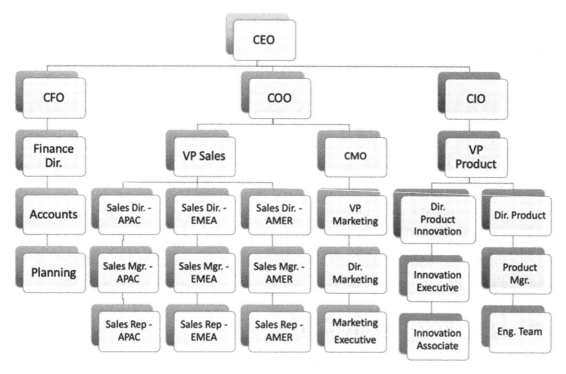

Figure 3-4. *GoC organizational chart*

Let's get back to Pamela. She hasn't had an opportunity to set up a role hierarchy in Salesforce and she is keen to do it. To start, she wants to set up the CEO's role.

Before she begins, she relies on her best practice know-how to delete all existing roles (default roles that come with a new Salesforce org) before creating a new set of role hierarchies. Then Pamela performs the following steps to create the CEO's role hierarchy:

1. She clicks Setup (gear icon) ➤ Setup ➤ ADMINISTRATION ➤ Users ➤ Roles.

2. She clicks Add Role below the company name, as shown in Figure 3-5.

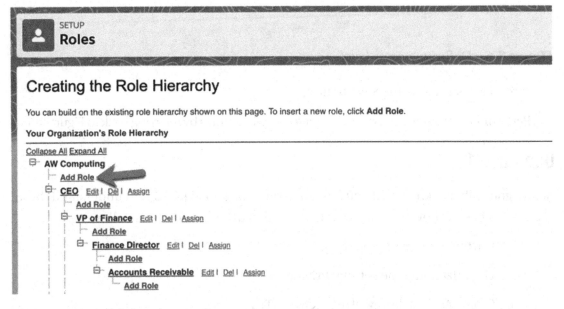

Figure 3-5. *Adding a new role*

3. She enters values for Label and Role Name, and makes sure to select an option in This role reports to. Pamela selects the company name.

4. Then she selects the CEO's access level to Contact, Opportunity, and Case, as shown in Figure 3-6.

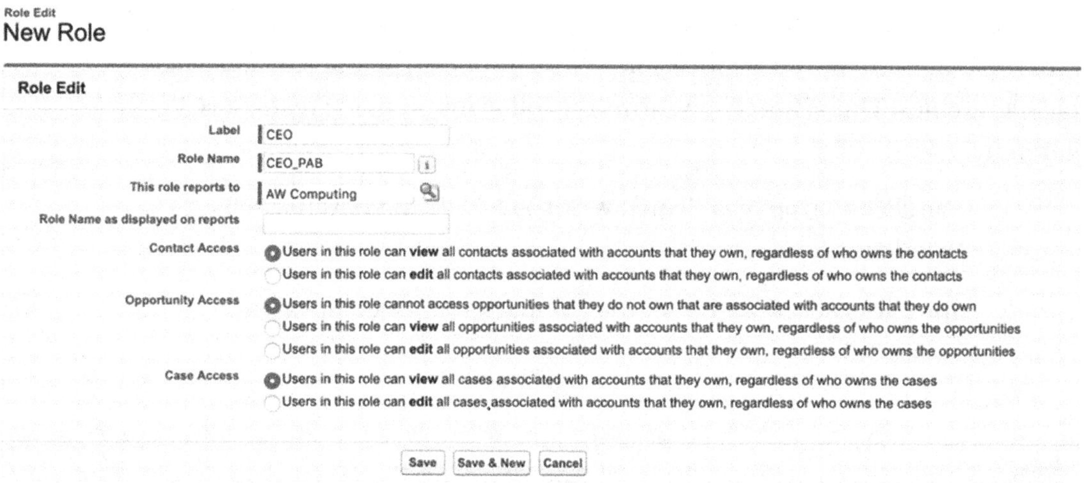

Role Edit
New Role

Role Edit

Label	CEO
Role Name	CEO_PAB
This role reports to	AW Computing
Role Name as displayed on reports	

Contact Access
- ● Users in this role can **view** all contacts associated with accounts that they own, regardless of who owns the contacts
- ○ Users in this role can **edit** all contacts associated with accounts that they own, regardless of who owns the contacts

Opportunity Access
- ● Users in this role cannot access opportunities that they do not own that are associated with accounts that they do own
- ○ Users in this role can **view** all opportunities associated with accounts that they own, regardless of who owns the opportunities
- ○ Users in this role can **edit** all opportunities associated with accounts that they own, regardless of who owns the opportunities

Case Access
- ● Users in this role can **view** all cases associated with accounts that they own, regardless of who owns the cases
- ○ Users in this role can **edit** all cases associated with accounts that they own, regardless of who owns the cases

[Save] [Save & New] [Cancel]

Figure 3-6. *Defining access level*

5. Last, she clicks the Save button.

Perform similar steps and create complete role hierarchies by referring back to Figure 3-5.

Use Case 1

Before going ahead, know that you'll need to refer back to Figure 3-4 to understand these use cases. Let's see how record access is granted to users based on the following:

1. Custom object: `Prospect__c`

2. Organization-wide setting: Private

3. `Grant Access Using Hierarchies`: True

Table 3-5 shows what happens when OWD is set to Private and `Grant Access Using Hierarchies` is set to True.

Table 3-5. *Record Access for Use Case 1*

Role	Access All Records	Access All Records Owned by Users Assigned to a Role	Access Records: Self-owned and Those Owned by Users below in the Role Hierarchy	Access Records: Self-owned Records Only
CEO	✓			
Chief Financial Officer (CFO)			✓ (Records owned by CFO and record owned by users in the role hierarchy below CFO)	
Sales Rep-Europe, the Middle East, and Africa (EMEA)				✓
Innovation Associate				✓
Dir. Product			✓ (Records owned by the director and by users below in the role hierarchy	
Users with no role				✓

In Table 3-5, access is granted as follows:

1. The CEO gets complete access (read, edit, delete, and share) to all records in the organization that has an assigned user. As a result, if a role is not assigned to a user, then neither the CEO nor anyone else in the organization can see records owned by that user.

2. The CFO and CIO are not able to access each other's records even though they are at the same level.

3. The CFO gets complete access (read, edit, delete, and share) to records owned by her and those owned by users in the Finance Dir, Accounts, and Planning roles.

4.   Sales Rep-EMEA and Innovation Associate can see only those records assigned/owned by them.

5.   Dir. Product gets complete access (read, edit, delete, and share) to records owned by him and those owned by users in the Product Mgr. and Eng. Team roles.

Use Case 2

Now let's tweak the scenario and change `Grant Access Using Hierarchies` to False (Table 3-6). Then, let's see how record access is granted to users based on the following:

1.   Custom object: `Prospect__c`

2.   Organization-wide setting: Private

3.   `Grant Access Using Hierarchies`: False

Table 3-6. *Record Access for Use Case 2*

Role	Access All Records	Access All Records Owned by Users Assigned to a Role	Access Records: Self-owned and Those Owned by Users below in the Role Hierarchy	Access Records: Self-owned Records Only
CEO				✓
CFO				✓
Sales Rep-EMEA				✓
Innovation Associate				✓
Dir. Product				✓
Users with no role				✓

It's as simple as that! When `Grant Access Using Hierarchies` is set to False, users only see those records they own. Period.

Use Case 3

Let's tweak the scenario again. This time, let's change OWD to Public Read Only and see how record access is granted to users based on the following (Table 3-7):

1. Custom object: `Prospect__c`

2. Organization-wide setting: Public Read Only

3. `Grant Access Using Hierarchies`: True

Table 3-7. *Record Access for Use Case 3*

Role	Access All Records	Access All Records Owned by Users Assigned to a Role	Access Records: Self-owned and Those Owned by Users below in the Role Hierarchy	Access Records: Self-owned Records Only
CEO	✓			
CFO	✓			
Sales Rep-EMEA	✓			
Innovation Associate	✓			
Dir. Product	✓			
Users with no role	✓			

Because OWD is the baseline setting, if it is set to Public Read Only, all users are able to see each other's records regardless of whether they are assigned a role.

Use Case 4

Let's look at another scenario and see how record view, edit, delete, and share capabilities work based on the following (Table 3-8):

1. Custom object: `Prospect__c`

2. Organization-wide setting: Private

3. `Grant Access Using Hierarchies:` True

Table 3-8. *Record Access for Use Case 4*

Role	Read	Edit	Delete	Share
CEO	Records CEO owns and those owned by users below the CEO in the role hierarchy	Records CEO owns and those owned by users below the CEO in the role hierarchy	Records CEO owns and those owned by users below CEO in the role hierarchy	Records CEO owns and those owned by users below CEO in the role hierarchy
CFO	Records CFO owns and those owned by users in the Finance Dir, Accounts, and Planning roles.	Records CFO owns and those owned by users in the Finance Dir, Accounts, and Planning roles.	Records CFO owns and those owned by users in the Finance Dir, Accounts, and Planning roles.	Records CFO owns and those owned by users in the Finance Dir, Accounts, and Planning roles.
Sales Rep-EMEA	Only records Sales Rep-EMEA owns	Only records Sales Rep-EMEA owns	Only records Sales Rep-EMEA owns	Only records Sales Rep-EMEA owns
Innovation Associate	Only records Innovation Associate owns	Only records Innovation Associate owns.	Only records Innovation Associate owns	Only records Innovation Associate owns
Dir. Product	Records Dir. Product owns and those owned by users in the Product Mgr. and Eng. Team roles	Records Dir. Product owns and those owned by users in the Product Mgr. and Eng. Team roles.	Records Dir. Product owns and those owned by users in the Product Mgr. and Eng. Team roles	Records Dir. Product owns and those owned by users in the Product Mgr. and Eng. Team roles
Users with no role	Only records they own	Only records they own	Only records they own	Only records they own

Because OWD is the baseline setting, when it is set to Private, users are able to access records they own and those owned by users below them in the role hierarchy.

Use Case 5

In the next scenario, let's take a look at how record view, edit, delete, and share capabilities work based on the following (Table 3-9):

1. Custom object: `Prospect__c`

2. Organization-wide setting: Public Read Only

3. `Grant Access Using Hierarchies:` True

Table 3-9. *Record Access for Use Case 5*

Role	Read	Edit	Delete	Share
CEO	All records	Records CEO owns and those owned by users below in the role hierarchy	Records CEO owns and those owned by users below in the role hierarchy	Records CEO owns and those owned by users below in the role hierarchy
CFO	All records	Records CFO owns and those owned by users in the Finance Dir, Accounts, and Planning roles	Records CFO owns and those owned by users in the Finance Dir, Accounts, and Planning roles	Records CFO owns and those owned by users in the Finance Dir, Accounts, and Planning roles
Sales Rep-EMEA	All records	Only records Sales Rep-EMEA owns	Only records Sales Rep-EMEA owns	Only records Sales Rep-EMEA owns
Innovation Associate	All records	Only records Innovation Associate owns	Only records Innovation Associate owns	Only records Innovation Associate owns
Dir. Product	All records	Records Dir. Product owns and those owned by users in the Product Mgr. and Eng. Team roles	Records Dir. Product owns and those owned by users in the Product Mgr. and Eng. Team roles	Records Dir. Product owns and those owned by users in the Product Mgr. and Eng. Team roles.
Users with no role	All records	Only records they own	Only records they own	Only records they own

When OWD is Public Read Only and `Grant Access Using Hierarchies` is True, then, regardless of whether a role hierarchy is used in an org, all users are able to view each other's records (assuming they have Read access on the object via their profile). Furthermore, users can edit, delete, and share only those records they own or are owned by users below them in the role hierarchy.

Use Case 6

Let's look at another scenario and see how record view, edit, delete, and share capabilities work (Table 3-10) with the following parameters:

1. Custom object: `Prospect__c`

2. Organization-wide setting: Public Read/Write

3. `Grant Access Using Hierarchies`: True

Table 3-10. *Record Access for Use Case 6*

Role	Read	Edit	Delete	Share
CEO	All records	All records	Records CEO owns and records owned by users below in the role hierarchy	Records CEO owns and records owned by users below in the role hierarchy
CFO	All records	All records	Records CFO owns and records owned by users in the Finance Dir, Accounts, and Planning roles, and below in the role hierarchy	Records CFO owns and records owned by users in the Finance Dir, Accounts, and Planning roles, and below in the role hierarchy
Sales Rep-EMEA	All records	All records	Only records Sales Rep-EMEA owns	Only records Sales Rep-EMEA owns
Innovation Associate	All records	All records	Only records Innovation Associate owns	Only records Innovation Associate owns
Dir. Product	All records	All records	Records Dir. Product owns and records owned by users in the Product Mgr. and Engineering Team roles, and below in the role hierarchy	Records Dir. Product owns and records owned by users in the Product Mgr. and Engineering Team roles, and below in the role hierarchy
Users with no role	All records	All records	Only records they own	Only records they own

As shown in Table 3-10, when OWD is set to Public Read/Write and, because it is a baseline setting, even though users may not be below in the role hierarchy or may not have a role assigned to them, they are still able to read and edit all records.

Use Case 7

Let's look at another scenario and see how record view, edit, delete, and share capabilities work (Table 3-11) with the following parameters:

1. Custom object: `Prospect__c`

2. Organization-wide setting: Public Read/Write

3. `Grant Access Using Hierarchies`: False

Table 3-11. *Record Access for Use Case 7*

Role	Read	Edit	Delete	Share
CEO	All records	All records	Only records CEO owns	Only records CEO owns
CFO	All records	All records	Only records CFO owns	Only records CFO owns
Sales Rep-EMEA	All records	All records	Only records Sales Rep-EMEA owns	Only records Sales Rep-EMEA owns
Innovation Associate	All records	All records	Only records Innovation Associate owns	Only records Innovation Associate owns
Dir. Product	All records	All records	Only records Dir. Product owns	Only records Dir. Product owns
Users with no Role	All records	All records	Only records they own	Only records they own

In this scenario, OWD is Public Read/Write, but Grant Access Using Hierarchies is set to False. As a result, users are not able to delete or share records owned by users below them in the role hierarchy, assuming they have CRED access on the object via profile.

I hope these use cases help you get a grip on the concepts of role hierarchy and OWD. If yes, awesome! You are making good progress! If still in doubt, no worries! Just reread and ponder these settings; try to visualize different scenarios. Later, make sure you perform a series of tests in your developer org.

Record-sharing Capabilities

So far, we've looked at record accessibility based on role hierarchy and OWD. Sometimes, you may need to share records with users that are *across* in the role hierarchy, *not below*. Here are a few examples of this:

1. The COO wants to access all records owned by the CFO. They both are at the same level as far as the role hierarchy goes. In this case, sharing needs to take place across and not below.

2. The CIO wants to share a few records, owned by the CIO, with the Chief Marketing Officer (CMO).

3. The company wants to share all records owned by Sales Dir. APAC with Sales Dir. EMEA.

Sharing rules are used to open up record access to groups of users, roles, or roles and subordinates notwithstanding the OWD setting. The sharing rule can't be used to restrict record access. Salesforce has the following types of sharing rules:

- **Manual sharing**: A Sharing button is enabled on the record detail page if OWD is set to Private or Public Read Only for any object. The record owners, or users, higher in the role hierarchy can share records with other users on a one-off basis.

- **Criteria-based sharing**: This rule allows system administrators to write a rule based on field values in a record. This is very helpful when you want to share a particular type of record with someone—for example, sharing all leads for Mumbai with Sales Rep-Asia–Pacific (APAC). You can have a maximum of 50 criteria-based sharing rules per object.

- **Owner-based sharing**: This rule allows system administrators to write a rule based on the owner of a record—for example, share all leads owned by users in role Sales Rep-EMEA with users in roles Sales Rep–North, Central and South America (AMER).

- **Apex-managed sharing**: This rule gives you the flexibility to handle complex business scenarios using Apex. For example, you have a field on the Lead object known as Potential Owner (User lookup). When this field is populated, you want to share the Lead record with the potential owner. This kind of scenario is handled easily through the Apex-managed sharing rule. You can either write Apex Trigger or Flow with Process Builder to handle this type of scenario. To access sharing objects programmatically, you must use the shared object associated with the standard or custom object you want to share.

Manual Sharing: Share Records on a One-off Basis

A Sharing button is enabled on the record detail page if OWD is set to Private or Public Read only for any object. The record owner, or users that are higher in the role hierarchy, can share records with other users on a one-off basis. Currently, Lightning Experience doesn't support the manual-sharing feature. Therefore, if you want to use manual sharing, switch back to Salesforce Classic. Currently, the Lead object's OWD is set as Private.

Let's go back to another business scenario with Pamela Kline. At this point she is well versed in role hierarchy, OWD, and sharing settings, and has set up role hierarchies successfully for GoC. Now she wants to share records manually with user Brent Bassi by leveraging the manual-sharing feature. Brent Bassi currently has Read/Write access.

Pamela does the following to meet the new requirement using manual sharing:

1. She clicks the Sharing button, as shown in Figure 3-7, which directs her to a new window.

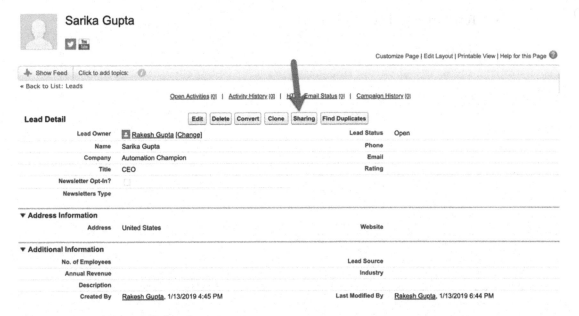

Figure 3-7. *Manual sharing*

2. She clicks the Add button.

3. She then selects one of the following options to share records with
    Brent (Figure 3-8):

    - Customer Portal Users

    - Manager Subordinates Groups

    - Manager Groups

    - Partner Users

    - Personal Groups

    - Portal Roles

    - Portal Roles and Subordinates

    - Public Groups

    - Roles

    - Roles and Internal Subordinates

    - Roles, Internal and Portal Subordinates

    - Territories

    - Territories and Subordinates

    - Users

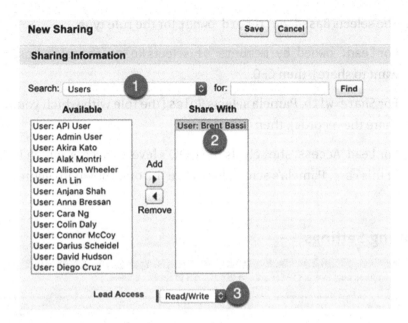

Figure 3-8. *Selects an option to share records*

4. Last, she clicks the Save button.

Owner-based Sharing: A Way to Share Records Automatically

Pamela is given a new task: share all records owned by the CFO with the COO, and make sure the records between the CFO and the COO continue to be shared going forward. Currently, the Lead object OWD is set to Private.

Pamela performs the following steps to conquer this task using owner-based sharing:

1. She navigates to Setup (gear icon) ➤ Setup ➤ SETTINGS ➤ Security ➤ Sharing Settings.

2. She locates the Lead Sharing Rules list.

3. Pamela clicks the New button to create a new rule and is redirected to a new window where she must enter the label, rule name, and description. As a good practice, Pamela always writes a description so other administrators or developers can understand why she created this rule.

    a. She selects `Based on record owner` for the rule type.

    b. For `Lead: owned by members of`, selects `Roles` (the role whose records you want to share), then `CFO`.

    c. For `Share with`, Pamela selects `Roles` (the role with which you want to share the records), then `COO`.

    d. For `Lead Access`, she selects the COO's level of access, which is Read Only in this case. Pamela's screen looks like the one shown in Figure 3-9.

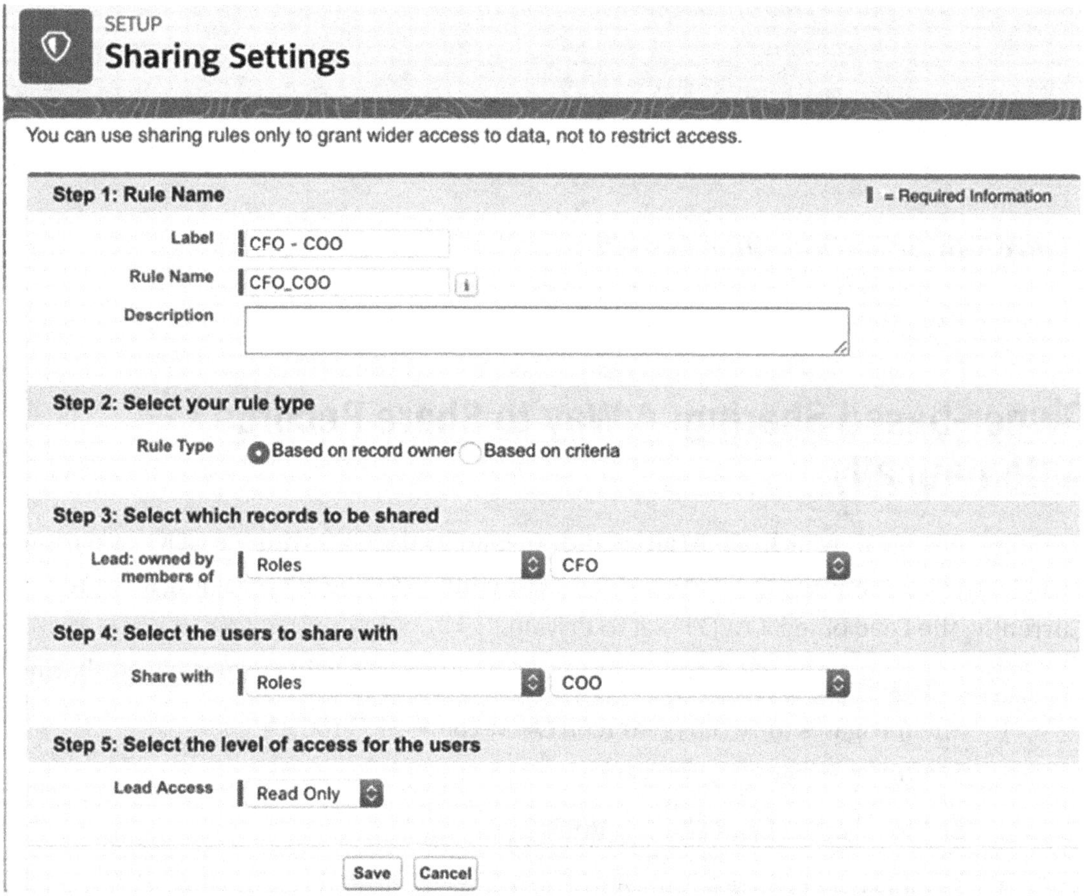

Figure 3-9. *Defining owner-based sharing*

4.   Last, she clicks the `Save` button.

After Pamela clicks the Save button, Salesforce recalculates the sharing settings. The requested changes are put into effect only after Salesforce is done recalculating the sharing settings.

Apex-managed Sharing: A Way to Manage Complex Sharing in Seconds

When all other sharing rules can't fulfill your requirements, then you should use Apex to share records. Apex enables you to handle complex business scenarios. For example, let's say you have a field on the Lead object known as Potential Owner (User lookup). The requirement is that when this field is populated, you share the Lead record with the potential owner. This kind of scenario is handled easily though Apex-managed sharing. You can write either Apex Trigger or Flow with Process Builder to handle this type of scenario. To access shared objects programmatically, you must specify the shared object whose records you want to share. We study Flow and Process Builder to create Apex-managed sharing in Chapter 7.

Deferring Sharing Calculations: Postpone Automatic Sharing Recalculation

Natively, every single change to the role hierarchy, groups, sharing rules, territory hierarchy, user roles, team membership, and ownership of records triggers sharing recalculations automatically. To suspend recalculation temporarily after making bulk changes, you have to "raise a ticket" with Salesforce. By so doing, you can make the changes and then run sharing recalculations at a time when it is least disruptive to your users. Let's look at this concept more closely.

For instance, if you are modifying OWD for an object, such as from Public Read Only to Public Read/Write, your changes take effect only after Salesforce runs a recalculation process. Recalculation may take minutes or hours to complete, depending on your org's data volume and customization. Similarly, if you modify a user's role, Salesforce runs all sharing rules again! For each update, Salesforce recalculates all access rights and sharing rules. As a result, if a user owns a lot of accounts and other records, the recalculation will take a long time to complete. If the recalculation runs in the background, then you won't be able to create new sharing rules or modify any security settings (such as OWD or the sharing rule) for that specific object in Salesforce (Figure 3-10).

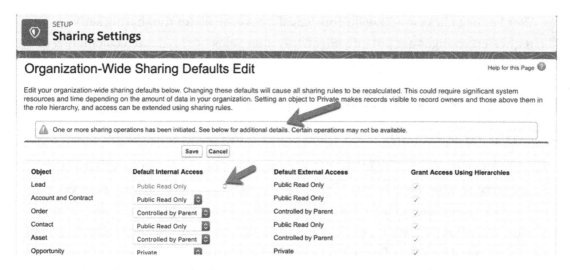

Figure 3-10. *Sharing recalculation message*

To avoid this snag, you have to enable the Defer Sharing Calculations feature by raising a support ticket with Salesforce (Figure 3-11). If you have an object that uses sharing and happens to have a large volume of records, and you need to make bulk changes (such as a periodical realignment requiring a hierarchy change) on that object, then deferring automatic sharing calculations is your best bet. When Defer Sharing Calculations is enabled by support, you can suspend the automatic sharing recalculation temporarily and run it when it is least disruptive to your users.

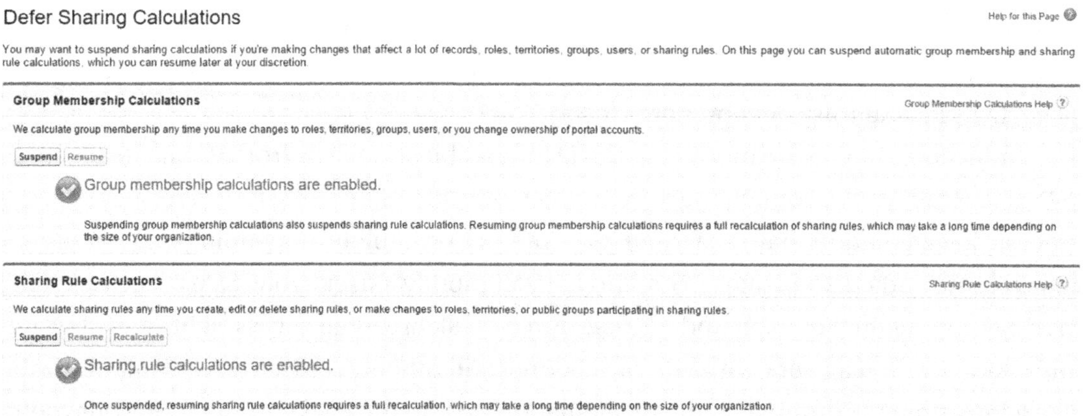

Defer Sharing Calculations   Help for this Page

You may want to suspend sharing calculations if you're making changes that affect a lot of records, roles, territories, groups, users, or sharing rules. On this page you can suspend automatic group membership and sharing rule calculations, which you can resume later at your discretion.

Group Membership Calculations   Group Membership Calculations Help

We calculate group membership any time you make changes to roles, territories, groups, users, or you change ownership of portal accounts.

[Suspend] [Resume]

Group membership calculations are enabled.

Suspending group membership calculations also suspends sharing rule calculations. Resuming group membership calculations requires a full recalculation of sharing rules, which may take a long time depending on the size of your organization.

Sharing Rule Calculations   Sharing Rule Calculations Help

We calculate sharing rules any time you create, edit or delete sharing rules, or make changes to roles, territories, or public groups participating in sharing rules.

[Suspend] [Resume] [Recalculate]

Sharing rule calculations are enabled.

Once suspended, resuming sharing rule calculations requires a full recalculation, which may take a long time depending on the size of your organization.

Figure 3-11. *Defer sharing calculations to postpone automatic sharing recalculation*

To summarize, OWD, role hierarchies, and sharing rules are tools that enable record sharing with users. Profiles and permission sets are used to control users' ability to perform action on these records, such as the ability to delete records owned by users who do not have delete permission through either profiles or permission sets. In some cases, profiles and permission sets bypass OWD, role hierarchies, and sharing rules.

Profiles: A Way to Control Actions Users Can Take on a Record

Profiles are a way to customize the overall Salesforce experience. They are used to define data security by granting object and field-level permissions that decide the set of fields users can access and the ability to perform actions on records. Profiles have certain permissions that can be used to grant, restrict, or bypass user access. Role hierarchies with OWD and sharing rules decide record-level access. Profiles determine which records (in terms of fields) users can see and actions they can perform.

Different Types of Profiles

There are two types of profiles in Salesforce:

1. **Standard**: Out-of-the box profile built into any Salesforce org. Standard profiles cannot be deleted.

2. **Custom**: Created by cloning a standard profile

The major difference between standard and custom profiles is that some parts of the standard profile can't be edited. For example, a standard profile's system, app, and object permissions can't be changed. Unlike custom profiles, which can be deleted if users are not assigned to them, standard profiles cannot be deleted.

Profiles contain system and object-specific permissions that override OWD:

- **View All Data:** This is a *system permission* that can be used to override OWD. For example, if we grant View All Data permission to users with the Marketing Executive role, then they can *view all records from all objects* regardless of their role or OWD.

- **Modify All Data**: This is a *system permission* that can be used to override OWD. For example, if we grant Modify All Data permission to users with the Marketing Executive role, then they can *modify all records from all objects* regardless of their role or OWD.

- **View All**: This is an *object-specific permission* that can be granted for each object manually. For example, if we grant View All permission to users with the Innovation Associate role for the Lead object, then they can *view all records of the Lead object* regardless of their role or OWD.

- **Modify All**: This is an *object-specific permission* that can be granted for each object manually. For example, if we grant Modify All permission to users with the Innovation Associate role, then they can *modify all records of the Lead object* regardless of their role or OWD.

As a rule of thumb, always create a custom profile by cloning it from a standard Read Only profile. The reason behind this is that the Read Only profile comes with minimal permission that can be modified easily.

Permission Sets

In Salesforce, users can have one, *and only one*, profile assigned to them. For example, Michelle White works as the COO at GoC. In the coming week, CFO Shannon Zadnowicz plans to go on a vacation for two weeks. As a result, Michelle will have to cover Shannon by performing the duties of COO and CFO. Therefore, Michelle will need more access in Salesforce to perform both the duties concomitantly. Because it is not possible to assign two profiles to a user, we have to grant more access to Michelle via permission sets.

Permission sets allow a system administrator to grant a group of settings and permissions to users beyond the users' existing profile. Via permission sets, the administrator can grant users access to various apps and functions their profile currently does not include. The settings available in permission sets are similar to profiles, but they extend users' functional access without changing their profiles.

Settings That Can Be Granted through Permission Sets

The following is a list of major settings that can be granted to users via permission sets:

- **Assigned apps**: Grants access to assigned apps.

- **Object settings**: Grants the following permissions on an object:

  - Tab settings

  - Record-type settings

  - Object permissions

  - Field-level permissions

- **App permissions**: Grants *specific permissions* to users within an app.

- **Apex class and Visualforce page access**: Grants Apex classes and Visualforce page access to users.

- **Service providers**: Grants access to a service provider when single sign-on is enabled.

- **Custom permission**: Grants permission to access custom processes and apps.

- **System permissions**: Defines permissions that apply across apps, such as View Encrypted Field, Modify All Data, and so on.

At runtime, user access is determined by the combined permissions granted via profiles *and* permission sets.

Granting Object Access

Using profiles and permission sets, a system administrator controls actions users can perform on a record.

Let's revisit Pamela Kline in another scenario. Currently, users with the role Sales Rep-APAC do not have permission to delete the records they own. As a result, Pamela receives a requirement to grant delete access to the following users (3 of 20) from the Sales Rep-APAC profile:

- Rakesh Gupta

- Sarika Gupta

- Munira Majmundar

To manage this requirement, Pamela uses permission sets instead of creating a new profile for the three Sales Rep-APAC users. In the future, the same the permission set can be used for other users from any other, or the same, profile.

Pamela performs the following steps to meet this new requirement:

1. Pamela clicks Setup (gear icon) ➤ Setup ➤ ADMINISTRATION ➤ Users ➤ Permission Sets and then clicks the New button.

2. She is redirected to a new screen where she enters the label, API name, and description. She also selects User License from the drop-down menu and leaves it blank.

3. Pamela clicks the Save button.

4. Under the Apps section, Pamela clicks Object Settings and selects the Leads object.

5. Pamela clicks Edit and navigates to Object Permissions.

6. She selects Delete permission, as shown in Figure 3-12. When she does this, the Read and Edit permissions are selected automatically by the system.

Object Permissions

Permission Name	Enabled
Read	☑
Create	☐
Edit	☑
Delete	☑
View All	☐
Modify All	☐

Figure 3-12. *Permissions that control use access for an object*

7. Pamela clicks the Save button.

8. She assigns the permission set to the users stipulated in the business requirement.

Note   To learn more about assigning a permission set to users, take a look at this Trailhead module: `https://trailhead.salesforce.com/en/content/` `learn/modules/wave_enable_setup/wave_set_up_permissions`.

If you plan to assign a permission set to all users who have the same user license type, the best practice is to associate that user license with the permission set. But, if you plan to assign a permission set to users with different user licenses (or users who might have different licenses in the future), it is probably best to create a permission set without user license type.

Managing Field-level security

So far, we've examined record-level accessibility, identifying which records are accessible by users, including OWD, role hierarchies, and sharing rules. Now let's switch to studying field visibility.

Data are the new gold. And therefore, the importance of safeguarding and nurturing your customers' or prospects' data is difficult to overstate, for this is the path to gaining customer and prospect trust, acquisition, and retention. Data security is critical to preventing data breaches. In every CRM, there are some key fields a business may want to hide from all users, such as Social Security number, bank details, a tax ID, and so on. Salesforce allows system administrators to use field-level security to hide fields or make them Read Only for specific profiles. There are four different ways to set field-level security:

1. Through a profile

2. Through a permission set

3. From an object field

4. Via field accessibility

Through a Profile

Remember, at runtime, user access is determined by the combined permissions granted via profiles *and* permission sets. Let's see how we set field-level security at the profile level by giving Pamela Kline a new task. She must hide the `Birthdate` field on the `Contact` object from users assigned to the `Standard User` profile.

To meet her requirement, Pamela performs the following steps:

1. She clicks Setup (gear icon) ➤ Setup ➤ ADMINISTRATION ➤ Users ➤ Profiles and then System User profile.

2. Under the Apps section, Pamela clicks Object Settings and then selects the Contact object.

3. Pamela clicks Edit and navigates to the Field Permission section.

4. She removes Read(1) access and Edit(2) access from the Birthdate field, as shown in Figure 3-13.

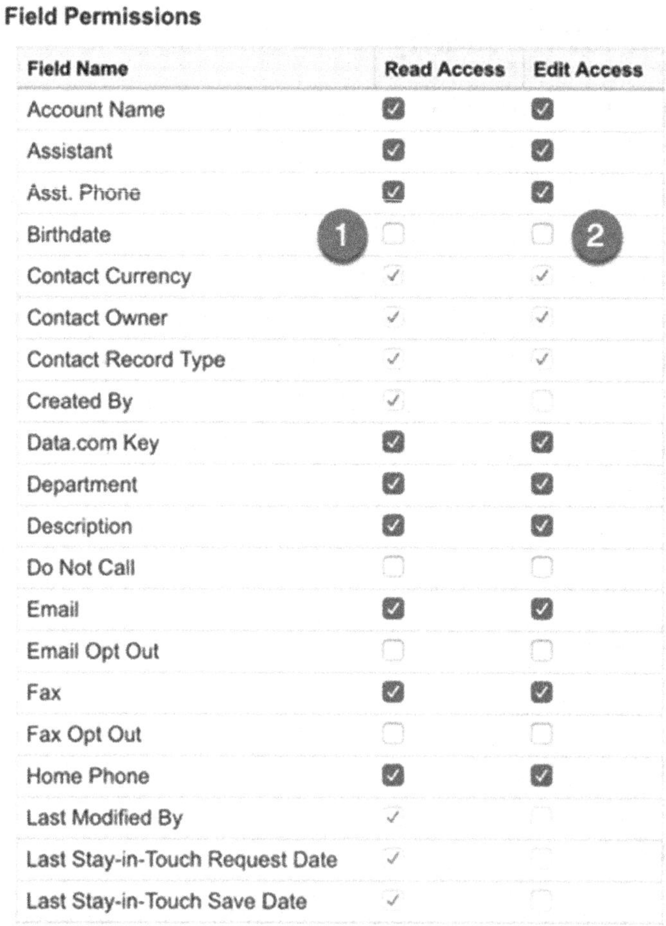

Field Permissions

Field Name	Read Access	Edit Access
Account Name	☑	☑
Assistant	☑	☑
Asst. Phone	☑	☑
Birthdate	☐ ①	② ☐
Contact Currency	✓	✓
Contact Owner	✓	✓
Contact Record Type	✓	✓
Created By	✓	☐
Data.com Key	☑	☑
Department	☑	☑
Description	☑	☑
Do Not Call	☐	☐
Email	☑	☑
Email Opt Out	☐	☐
Fax	☑	☑
Fax Opt Out	☐	☐
Home Phone	☑	☑
Last Modified By	✓	☐
Last Stay-in-Touch Request Date	✓	
Last Stay-in-Touch Save Date	✓	☐

Figure 3-13. *Field permissions are used to control field read/edit access*

5. She clicks the Save button.

Points to Remember

1. If you are changing the default access, such as from Public Read Only to Public Read/Write, your changes take effect *after Salesforce completes running the recalculation process.*

2. Users with Edit permission on the price books—granted via profiles or permission sets—get access to all price books, regardless of OWD.

3. When you select the `Grant Access Using Hierarchies` field, it provides access to people who are above the owner in the role hierarchy.

4. If your sharing model for related opportunities is Public Read Only then, a `Sharing` button may appear on an Account detail page even though your sharing model for Account is Public Read/Write.

5. It is not possible to include high-volume portal users in sharing rules because they don't have roles and can't be included in a public group.

6. The sharing rule is always used to open up access. If you want to restrict record access, you have to modify your org's OWD.

7. Salesforce doesn't allow anyone to delete the `Standard User` profile.

8. If you select the `Read Only` check box under object field-level security, then the `Visible` check box is selected automatically.

9. Make sure to enable field history tracking for a field if you want to track which users are changing field values and when they are doing so.

10. When working with object and field access, *the most restrictive setting wins.*

11. When working with record access, *the most permissive setting wins.*

12. To increase the limit on a sharing rule, raise a case with Salesforce support. By default, you can define up to 300 user sharing rules, including up to 50 criteria-based sharing rules.

13. The external access level for an object can't be more permissive than the internal access level.

Hands-on Exercises

The following exercises will give you more practice with the platform, which ultimately will help you in gaining mastery of it, and also will assist you in preparing for the certification examination. Remember, these are hands-on exercises, and you can find the answers at the back of the book in the Appendix, but try to implement them in your Salesforce org, which is the primary goal of doing them.

1. Create a custom object known as Address (Address__c). Then, check OWD for this object under Security Setting. Test your knowledge by selecting one of the following options:

   a. Private

   b. Public Read/Write

   c. Public Full Access

   d. Public Read Only

2. Set OWD for Address (Address__c) in such a way that if users don't own a record in the Address object, then they can't access the record.

3. Dennis Williams, a system administrator at GoC, has to meet the following requirements for Address (Address__c):

   a. Address records can't be accessed by all users

      i. CEO: Can access all records

      ii. COO: Can access all records

      iii. Sales Rep-EMEA: Users in this role can access all records.

iv. Sales Rep-APAC: Two of 20 users in this role can access all records. The remaining cannot access a single record.

v. Sales Rep-AMER: Users in this role can access all records.

b. Pamela Kline, the system administrator, owns all records.

c. Users can only view, but cannot edit or delete, any record in the Address__c object.

4. Dennis Williams has a requirement to create a field to store Social Security numbers. He wants to make sure that only a system administrator and key users, including the following, can access the Social Security Number field:

a. Rakesh Gupta

b. Sarika Gupta

c. Munira Majmundar

5. Dennis has a requirement to share ten records, which are currently owned by VP Sales, with a user belonging to the Dir. Product role. What kind of sharing mechanism would you suggest to him? Select one of the following options:

a. OWD

b. Owner-based sharing

c. Manual sharing

d. Criteria-based sharing

e. Permission set

6. Dennis is having a hard time debugging one record-sharing problem. Please help him solve it. Here is the complete scenario:

a. Object: Address__c

b. OWD: Public Read/Write

c. Grant Access Using Hierarchies: True

d. Owned by system administrator

e. Company CEO (Rakesh Gupta) is not able to delete this record. Why?

7. Dennis is gradually grasping the concept of the sharing architecture. However, he is having a hard time debugging one record-sharing problem. Please help him solve it. Here is the complete scenario:

   a. Object: `Address__c`

   b. OWD: Public Read Only

   c. `Grant Access Using Hierarchies`: True

   d. Owned by system administrator

   e. Company CEO (Rakesh Gupta) is not able to edit the record. Why?

8. Dennis wants to implement opportunity management at GoC, but he is a bit confused with one of the requirements. Because you now have a better understanding of record sharing, please help him to select the appropriate sharing architecture to fulfill the following requirements:

   a. When the opportunity amount is greater than US$1,000,000, share the record with VP Product.

   b. However, autorevoke record access from VP Product if the opportunity amount drops to less than US$1,000,000.

9. Help Dennis select the appropriate object-level security for the `Lead` object where 3 of 20 Sales Rep-AMER users can create new Lead records, but the remaining 17 users can only view the Lead records. List all the Salesforce features that Dennis can use to solve this requirement.

10. Dennis has a new requirement to tackle: all users from in the Eng. Team role must be able to modify all records from the `Lead` object. What is your suggestion for Dennis to solve this requirement?

11. Dennis has a requirement to share leads that have an annual revenue of more than US$10,000,000 and belong to the London office. The owner is Shannon Zadnowicz, CFO at GoC. What is your recommendation, for Dennis, to solve this requirement?

12. Currently, all users can see all Lead records. Dennis receives a new requirement to make the following modifications:

    a. Except for users Rakesh Gupta and Munira Majmundar, all users can see all Lead records.

    b. Ban Rakesh Gupta and Munira Majmundar from accessing any records.

    How can Dennis meet this requirement?

13. Dennis is implementing account management at GoC and has a new requirement: only if users have access to the Account record can they also access related Contact records. Help Dennis fulfill this requirement.

14. Dennis has a new requirement: share the Lead record with Dir. Product, just for 48 hours, if the annual revenue is greater than US$100,000,000. Help Dennis fulfill this requirement.

Summary

In this chapter, we covered OWD and how it affects record accessibility, followed by an in-depth look at role hierarchies. We also studied various sharing rules available in Salesforce and reviewed the functionality of profiles and permission sets. Last, we looked at object and field-level security and their use cases. In Chapter 4, we take a deep dive into Lightning Experience customization.

CHAPTER 4

Customizing the User Interface

In Chapter 3, we studied the Salesforce sharing architecture, including OWD and role hierarchies. We saw how different real-world problems can be solved by using various sharing mechanisms. Last, we looked at how profiles and permission sets play a key role in handling object- and field-level security in Salesforce.

This chapter is divided into three sections: taking a deep dive into Lightning Experience; creating dynamic Lightning pages; and enabling custom buttons, links, and actions.

A Deep Dive into Lightning Experience

Unlike Salesforce Classic, the engine behind Lightning Experience is a user's device agnostic. What does that mean? Well, mobile use has been increasing exponentially—be it at the workplace or for personal use. Sales reps are now using mobile devices to find potential customers, use social media to connect with customers, and more. Lightning Experience mimics the way sales reps work on a mobile platform and thus provides a seamless experience across platforms.

Lightning Experience is a fresh and productive user interface. It is aimed at helping sales reps close more deals quickly by providing flexible, intuitive, and interactive tools. The tools enable the reps to focus on deals, customers, and activities that promise the greatest returns. The sophisticated Lightning Experience user interface, coupled with Einstein's predictive modeling, turbocharge sales rep productivity exponentially by enabling them to take the step at the right time, with the right customer, on the right deal.

93

© Rakesh Gupta 2020
R. Gupta, *Salesforce Platform App Builder Certification*, https://doi.org/10.1007/978-1-4842-5479-0_4

In addition to being faster, Lightning Experience enables system administrators to deliver a pleasant user experience by quickly building a Lighting page to suit a user's working style or needs. Lightning Experience uses a component-based design pattern. This means, to build a Lightning page, all you have to do is place components onto a page at the location of your choice! Let's go ahead and see what Lightning Experience looks like.

The Lightning Experience Navigation Menu

Similar to the navigation menu in Salesforce Classic, Lightning Experience also displays tabs across the top of the screen. Furthermore, with Lightning Experience, as with Classic, end users can customize the navigation menu to suit their working style and needs. Via the navigation menu, users can take the following actions (Figure 4-1):

- Switch apps via App Launcher.

- Identify the current app's name.

- Access recent records.

- Create new records.

Figure 4-1. *Lightning app navigation menu*

In addition, end users can customize the navigation menu (including reordering and adding/removing tabs) by adding the following items to the menu:

- Standard objects

- Custom objects

- Home tab

- Visualforce tabs

- Lightning component tabs

- Web tabs

- Canvas apps via Visualforce tabs

The App Launcher in Lightning Experience

As mentioned, Lightning Experience allows a user to switch between apps using App Launcher. Apps show up as large tiles under All Apps. The apps list can include standard apps, custom apps, and connected apps, such as G Suite. Other items, such as custom objects, tasks, events, and feeds, show up under All Items. Users can find apps by searching for the app name in the search box (1 in Figure 4-2) or by using the App Launcher (2 in Figure 4-2).

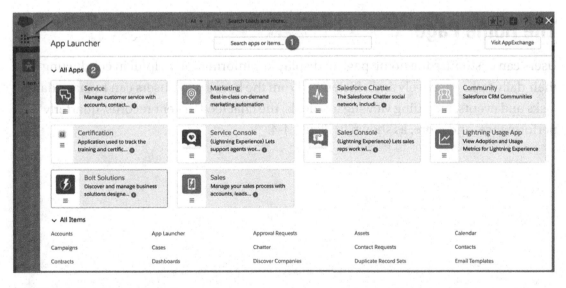

Figure 4-2.   *Access App Launcher*

In addition, users can also personalize the order of the apps on this page by dragging the tiles per their needs (Figure 4-3). However, be aware that a Salesforce administrator can override the app sort order set by users.

Figure 4-3. *Rearrange apps in Lightning*

The app menu lists all apps installed in the org. However, the apps users see in App Launcher and in the app menu may vary based on visibility settings and user permissions set on their profile.

The Home Page

Users can customize the home page to display key information helpful in conducting their daily tasks effectively and efficiently. From the home page, users can manage daily tasks and events, including viewing top deals, the chat feed, recent records, quarterly performance, and more, as shown in Figure 4-4.

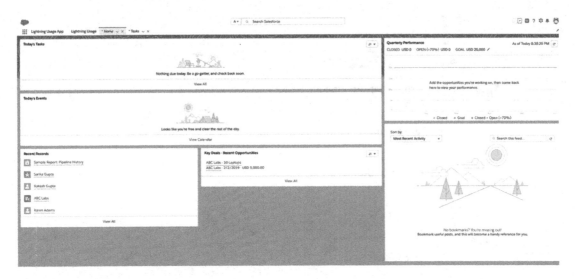

Figure 4-4. *Lightning home page*

Furthermore, unlike Classic, with Lightning Experience, users can remove the Home tab from a Lightning app. A Home tab is no longer mandatory!

Global Search

What happens if users have tons of records in Salesforce? How can they get what they need quickly? Well, global search is there to rescue these users!

Global search finds exactly what users are looking for by breaking a search term into small parts. The global search box is available at the top of every page in Lightning Experience. When users click the global search box, they see a drop-down of all recent items, as shown in Figure 4-5.

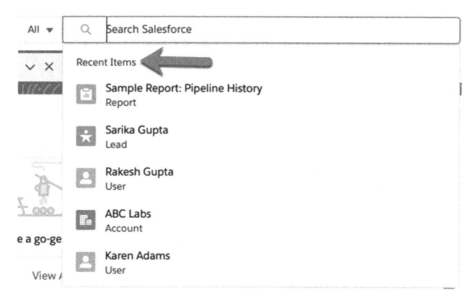

Figure 4-5. *Access global search*

If users start typing in the search box, the list updates dynamically with matches from all searchable objects. When users see what they are looking for, then they can select it quickly. As the example in Figure 4-6 shows, if a user types sari in the search box, the system shows all records that contain sari anywhere.

Figure 4-6. *Search on a partial word*

If users click the global search box from an object-specific view, like from a Leads page, then, the global search looks for leads based on the search string.

Creating Dynamic Lightning Pages

The beauty of Salesforce's Lightning Experience is that it allows users to create dynamic pages without writing a single line of code. Such features deliver a high level of sophistication and customization in Lightning Experience that is missing from Classic.

Controlling Component Visibility

Let's return to Robin Guzman, a Salesforce administrator at GoC. His basic understanding of Lightning Experience—how to navigate within it and create a Lightning page—has increased greatly. He created a Lightning record page (Lead Record page) for the Lead object and made it the org default (Figure 4-7).

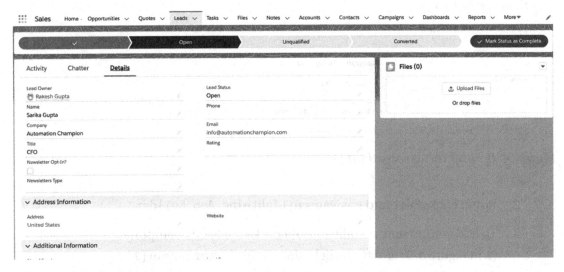

Figure 4-7. *Lead Lightning page*

Now he wants to learn how to make the Files component dynamic on the Leads record page based on the logged-in user. Specifically, he wants to hide the Files component from the system administrator.

Robin does the following to solve the preceding business requirement by leveraging the component visibility setting:

1. He navigates to Setup (gear icon) ➤ Setup ➤ Object Manager ➤ Lead ➤ Lightning Record Pages and locates the Lead record page (Figure 4-8).

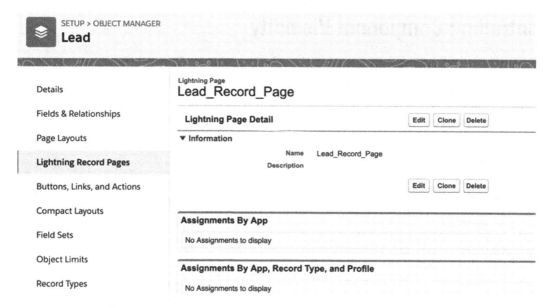

Figure 4-8. *Lightning record page*

2. Robin clicks Edit and navigates to Lightning App Builder.

3. To add component visibility, Robin clicks the Files component (1 in Figure 4-9) and then clicks the + Add Filter button (2 in figure 4-9), which is available under Set Component Visibility.

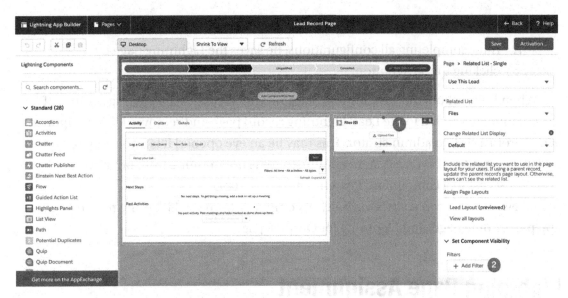

Figure 4-9. *Lightning App Builder*

4. This action redirects Robin to a new window, where he selects the filter type, field, operator, and value as follows:

   a. For `Filter Type`, she selects `Advanced`.

   b. For `Field`, he selects `Profile Name` by navigating to User ➤ Profile ➤ Name.

   c. For `Operator`, he selects `Not Equal`.

   d. For `Value`, he selects `System Administrator`.

5. In the end, Robin's screen looks look the one in Figure 4-10.

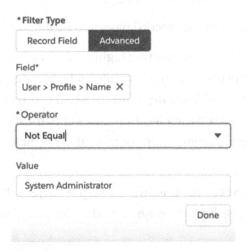

Figure 4-10. *Set component visibility*

6.   He clicks the Done button.

7.   After completing all configurations, he saves the Lightning page by clicking the Save button.

When Robin clicks the Save button, Salesforce recalculates the sharing settings of the components added to the Lead Lightning record page and removes Files component access from a system administrator. This may be an eye opener! It is important to know and understand that even a system administrator is not immune from not having visibility access to a component. Powerful indeed!

Likewise, users can control visibility of components on the Lightning record page, app page, home page, and Lightning for Outlook page.

Lightning Page Assignment

In Lightning Experience, users can set Lightning page assignments based on different parameters. For example, users can create multiple Lightning Lead record pages and then assign them based on the following parameters:

- Assign a page as an org default.

- Assign a page as the default for specific Lightning apps. For instance, users can have multiple Lead lightning pages based on different Lightning apps. Users can assign Lead record pages (Sales) to the Lightning Sales app. Similarly, they can assign Lead record pages (Service) to the Lightning Service app.

- Use a combination of app, record type, and profile.

Robin has now become a pro in creating Lightning record pages and knows how to show and hide components from them. He created a Lightning record page for Lead called Lead Record Page (Sales). Next he wants to assign this record page to the Sales app so that whenever users open the Lightning Sales app, they see this page for the Lead record. Robin performs the following steps to meet this requirement using the page visibility setting:

1.   He navigates to Setup (gear icon) ➤ Setup ➤ Object Manager ➤ Lead ➤ Lightning Record Pages and then locates Lead Record Page (Sales).

2. Robin clicks Edit and navigates to Lightning App Builder.

3. To add component visibility, he clicks the Activation button at the right-hand top corner. The system redirects Robin to a new window to set up the Lightning page assignment.

4. Robin clicks the APP DEFAULT tab and then the Assign as App Default button to set the Lightning page for the Lighting Sales app, as shown in Figure 4-11.

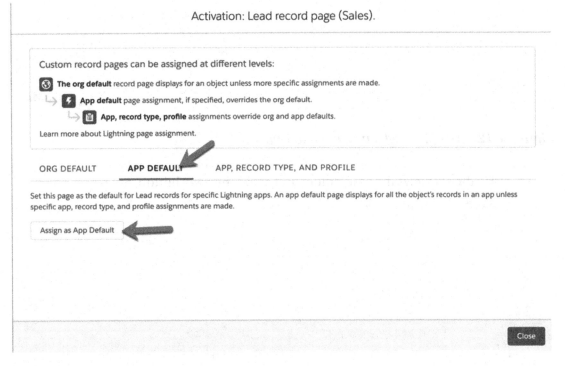

Figure 4-11. *Set Lightning page assignment*

5. Then he selects the app: Sales.

6. Robin clicks the Next button, as shown in Figure 4-12.

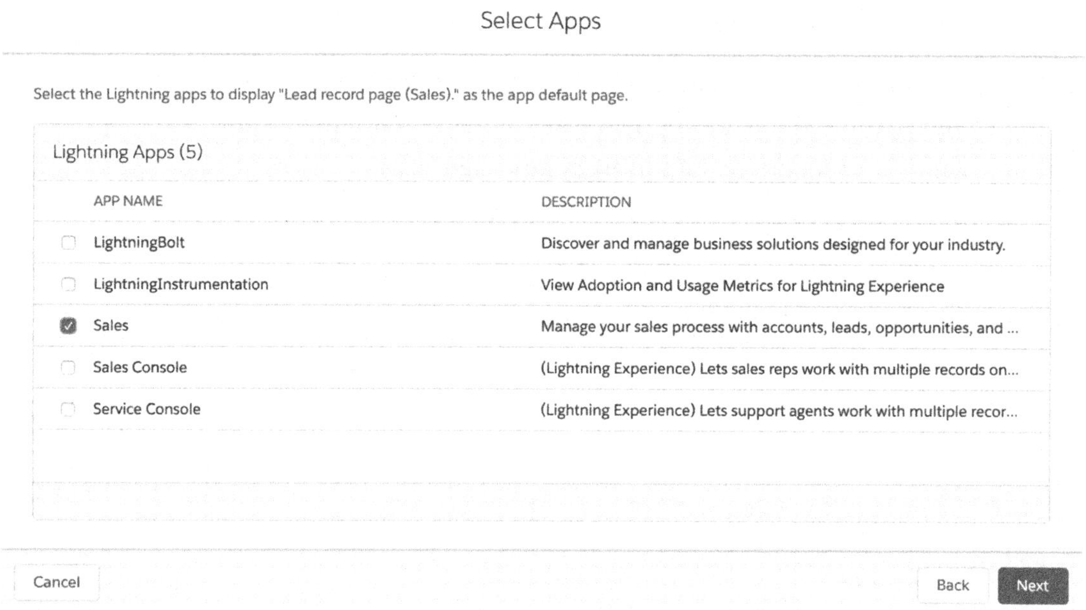

Select Apps

Select the Lightning apps to display "Lead record page (Sales)." as the app default page.

Lightning Apps (5)	
APP NAME	DESCRIPTION
☐ LightningBolt	Discover and manage business solutions designed for your industry.
☐ LightningInstrumentation	View Adoption and Usage Metrics for Lightning Experience
☑ Sales	Manage your sales process with accounts, leads, opportunities, and ...
☐ Sales Console	(Lightning Experience) Lets sales reps work with multiple records on...
☐ Service Console	(Lightning Experience) Lets support agents work with multiple recor...

Cancel   Back   Next

Figure 4-12. *Assign a Lightning page to apps*

7. He then reviews the assignment and clicks the Save button, as shown in Figure 4-13.

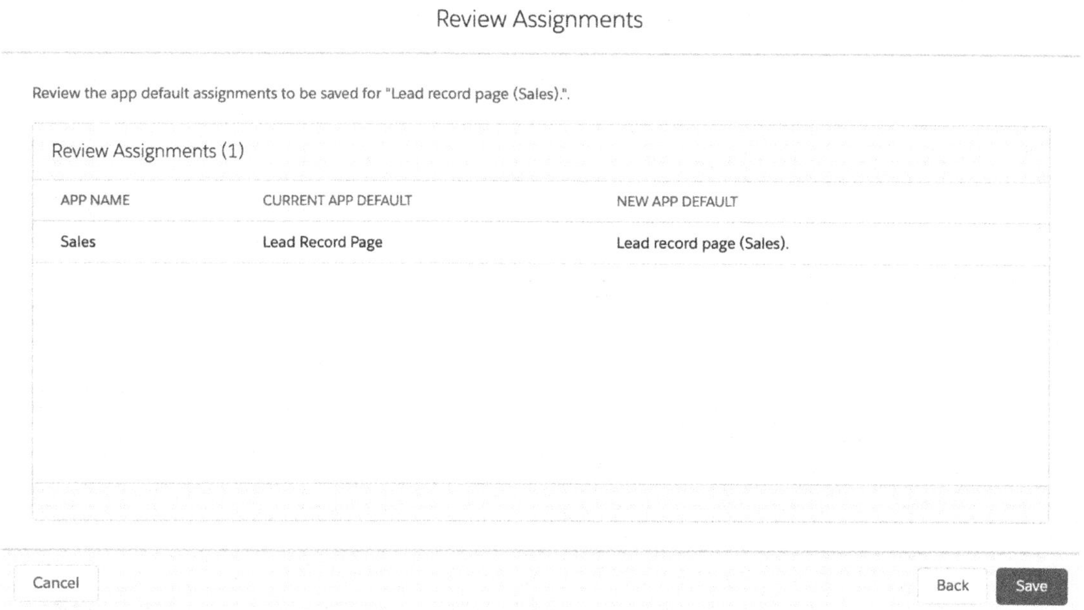

Review Assignments

Review the app default assignments to be saved for "Lead record page (Sales).".

Review Assignments (1)		
APP NAME	CURRENT APP DEFAULT	NEW APP DEFAULT
Sales	Lead Record Page	Lead record page (Sales).

Cancel   Back   Save

Figure 4-13. *Review the Lightning page assignment*

After Robin clicks the Save button, Salesforce recalculates the sharing settings and page assignment for the Lead object. Going forward, users will see the Lead Record Page (Sales) when they select the Lightning Sales app and open the Lead record.

Use Case for Custom Buttons and Links

Each business unit has its own set of requirements that may require specific configuration. For example, if users are responsible for managing vendors and they want to allow access to an Account page from outside the org (e.g., for a vendor management system), then Salesforce requires users to create a custom button or a link.

A custom button or a link allows users to integrate Salesforce data from external applications or data from a company's internal portal, for example. The ability to access Salesforce data from an external application—with a click of a button or a link—boosts user productivity several-fold.

In Lightning Experience, custom buttons and links, when added to a page layout, appear in different regions of a Lightning page. Here are the different types of custom buttons and links users can create in Salesforce:

- **List button**: Appears in a related list of an object's record page.

- **Detail page link**: Appears in the Links section of the details page of an object's record.

- **Detail page button**: Appears in the action menu in the highlight panel of an object's record page.

Let's rejoin Robin, who has just received a requirement to create a custom button on a Lead page to search a lead company using Google search. After clicking the button, it should open a Google search page and find details about the lead company.

Robin performs the following steps to meet this requirement by creating a custom button:

1. He navigates to Setup (gear icon) ➤ Setup ➤ Object Manager ➤ Lead ➤ Buttons, Links and Actions.

2. Robin clicks New Button or Link, which redirects him to a new window to set up a custom button. Once there, he works his way through by entering information as follows:

a. **Label**: Robin names her custom button Open Google Search.

b. **Name**: This field autopopulates based on the label.

c. **Description**: Robin writes some meaningful text so that other developers and administrators can understand easily why the custom button was created in the first place.

d. **Display Type**: He selects Detail Page Button.

e. **Behavior**: He selects Display in existing window without sidebar.

f. **Content Source**: He selects URL, then pastes the following URL into the large text box: https://www.google.com/search?q={!Lead.Company}.

In the end, Robin's screen looks like the one depicted in Figure 4-14.

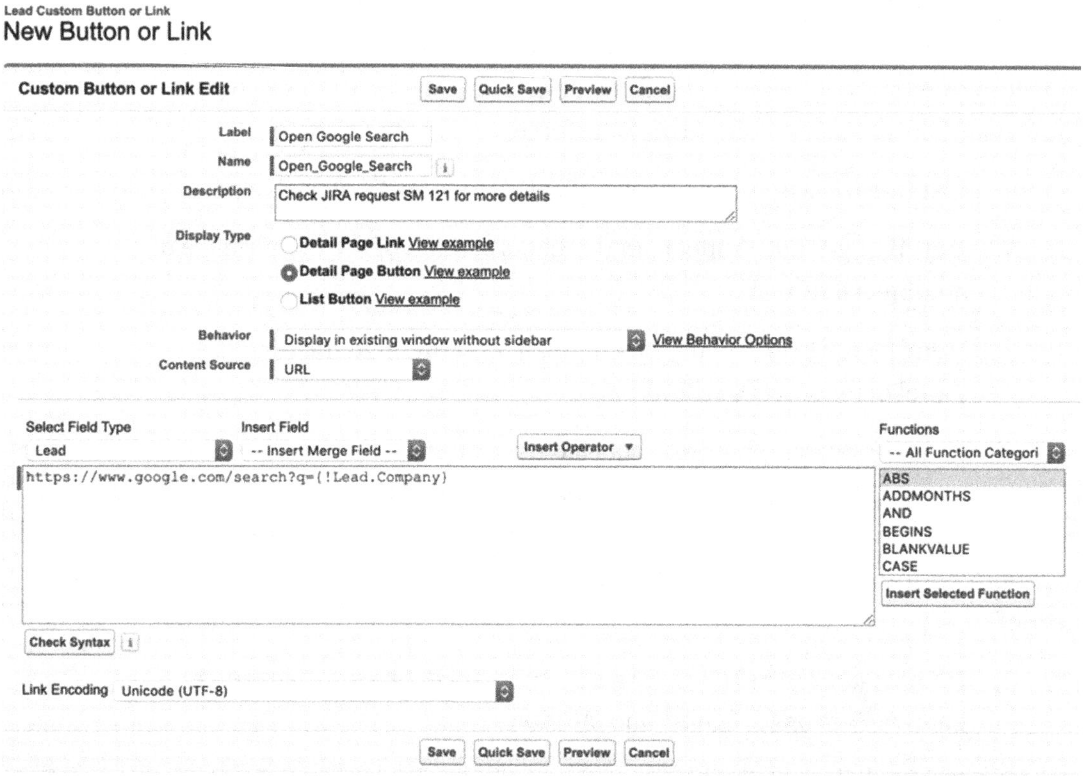

Figure 4-14. *Creating a custom button*

3. Robin clicks the Save button.

4. Next, he adds a new custom button to the Lead page layout by
    navigating to Setup (gear icon) ➤ Setup ➤ Object Manager ➤
    Lead ➤ Page layouts.

5. Then he clicks the Edit link and drags and drops the custom
    button Open Google Search to the Salesforce Mobile and
    Lightning Experience Actions section of the page layout, as shown
    in Figure 4-15.

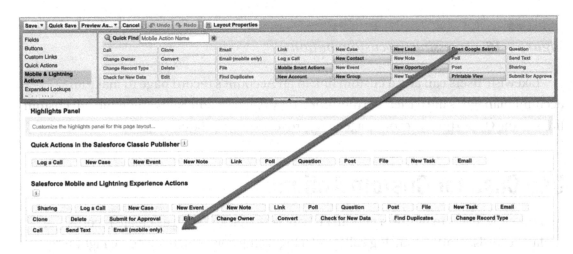

Figure 4-15. *Adding a button to Lightning Experience*

6. Robin clicks the Save button.

7. He makes sure to whitelist the https://www.goggle.com URL.

Going forward, the Open Google Search custom button is available in the Lead
record page's highlight panel, as shown in Figure 4-16.

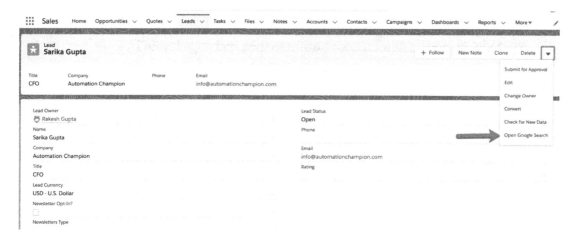

Figure 4-16. *Accessing the custom button*

Likewise, users can add a custom link to an Account's record page to make an account manager's life easier. Furthermore, they can also add Sales guideline pdf custom links to the Opportunity record page to improve a team's productivity.

Use Case for Custom Actions

Actions allow users to perform certain activity very quickly, such as create records, update records, send e-mail, log calls, call a Lightning component, execute Lightning Flow, and call a Visualforce page. With custom actions, users save precious time by getting quick access to important information. There are two types of actions available to users: object specific and global:

1. **Object-specific actions**: Object-specific actions have automatic relationships to other records. The actions let users quickly create or update records, send e-mail, log calls, call Lightning components, execute Lightning Flow, and call a Visualforce page in the context of a particular object. A few examples of object-specific actions include the following:

    a. Creating a custom action on Opportunity object to update Stage to Closed Lost, as shown in Figure 4-17.

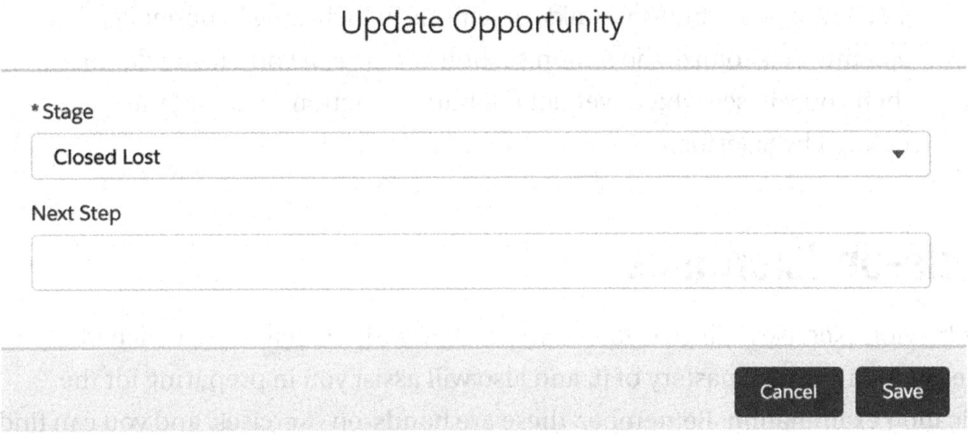

Update Opportunity

---

*Stage

| Closed Lost ▼ |

Next Step

| |

Cancel   Save

Figure 4-17. Updating the Opportunity object

    b. Creating a `Record Create` action (`Create Order`) from `Opportunity` without leaving the Opportunity record page.

2. **Global actions**: Users can create global actions in `Setup`, then put global actions anywhere on an object that supports actions. Using global actions, users can log calls, create records, send e-mail, call a Visualforce page, execute a Lightning component, and call Custom Canvas all without leaving the page.

In Chapter 6, we see how to use custom actions to call Lightning Flow.

Points to Remember

- Users can't personalize the navigation bar when it contains more than 50 items.

- When a system administrator removes an item from an app, that item remains in users' personalized navigation bars. Then, if they so choose, users can delete the item.

- Lightning apps aren't available in Classic.

- The object-specific `Send Email` action is only available on cases.

- To show custom buttons, links, or actions in Lightning Experience, you must customize the Action section of a page layout. If you do not, then you will see whichever default buttons, actions, and links are defined by Salesforce.

Hands-on Exercises

The following exercises will give you more practice with the platform, which ultimately will help you in gaining mastery of it, and also will assist you in preparing for the certification examination. Remember, these are hands-on exercises, and you can find the answers at the back of the book in the Appendix, but try to implement them in your Salesforce org, which is the primary goal of doing them.

1. Edit a Lightning record page of a Lead object and explore different components. Test out its role and functionality.

2. Create a custom button to open a Yahoo News page for Account.

3. Dennis Williams, a system administrator at GoC, has received the following requirements:

   - On an Account Lightning record page, hide the News component from those users that do not have Access Activities permission.

   How would you instruct Dennis to perform this task?

4. Dennis Williams has new requirements: create a quick action on the Lead object to update Status quickly to Unqualified, then add the quick action to all Lead record pages. How would you instruct Dennis to perform these tasks?

5. Create a custom Lightning app (named Sales Critical) and add the following tabs to it:

   - Home

   - Lead

   - Account

- Contact

- Opportunity

- Campaign

Then, list all your new findings, including app logo size, navigation style, and app personalization settings, and add a Utility Item section.

Summary

In this chapter, we looked at an overview of Lightning Experience, followed by an in-depth study of the dynamic record pages. We also examined custom buttons, links, and actions use cases with real-life examples. In Chapter 5, we take at deep dive into how to improve and enrich data quality in Salesforce.

CHAPTER 5

Improving and Enriching Data Quality

In Chapter 4, we looked at an overview of Lightning Experience and studied the dynamic record page. Last, we discussed use cases for custom buttons, links, and actions using real-life examples.

This chapter is comprised of two parts. The first part is divided into two sections; part two is divided into three sections.

In part one, the first section consists of an overview of record types; the second section takes a look at lookup filters and dependent lookups.

In part two, the first section consists of an overview of formula fields, the second section discusses a use case of a roll-up summary field, and the last section examines the best way to write enterprise-level validation rules using custom permissions.

Record Types: A Better Way to Handle Varied Business Processes

Record types play a key role in Salesforce implementation. Without having a good understanding of them, developers or architects may end up devising an incorrect solution or writing code, which may turn out to be a suboptimal solution.

For example, suppose there is a custom object Registrant that is being used to store event participants. Depending on the value in the Industry field, a marketing director wants to display different fields on a page layout, as shown in Table 5-1. If the value in the Industry field is Manufacturing, then the director wants to display additional fields on a page layout, such as Annual Income, Date of Birth, or Shift Hours. If, however, the value in the Industry field is anything other than Manufacturing, the director does not want to display the additional fields.

113

© Rakesh Gupta 2020
R. Gupta, *Salesforce Platform App Builder Certification*, https://doi.org/10.1007/978-1-4842-5479-0_5

Table 5-1. *Representation the Data Marketing Director Wants to Capture*

Manufacturing	Other
First Name	First Name
Last Name	Last Name
E-mail	E-mail
Event	Event
Industry (Manufacturing, Shipping, Consulting, and Other)	Industry (Manufacturing, Shipping, Consulting, and Other)
Phone	Phone
Annual Income*	
Date of Birth*	
Shift Hours*	

Now there are various ways to meet this requirement. For example, we can write *validation rules* that state that whenever the value in the Industry field is Manufacturing, make the three other fields required. This requires users to populate the fields before they can save the record.

Even if the validation rule works, it will create a negative user experience because the required fields, as a result of the value Manufacturing in the Industry field, would not have red asterisk attached to it.

Figure 5-1 demonstrates how developers can make fields required based on the value in the Industry field. The aforementioned approach (Figure 5-1) has the following issues:

1. Right off the bat, it creates a negative user experience because the required fields (only when the value in the Industry field is Manufacturing) would not display a red asterisk next to it!

2. Second, what happens if users select a value other than Manufacturing in the Industry field? In such a scenario, they would be able to *skip entering the data in the aforementioned required fields because the validation rule would not trigger* if the value in the Industry field is anything other than Manufacturing. This situation creates a big dent in achieving, and maintaining, data integrity—to say the least!

> To avoid a negative user experience or avoid compromising data integrity, developers and architects have to write a complex validation rule.

3. The validation rule route displays unnecessary fields on a page layout when a value other than Manufacturing is in the Industry field. In such a scenario, fields like Annual Income, Date of Birth, or Shift Hours would gobble up page layout real estate without adding any value—not to mention delivering a suboptimal user experience.

4. Last but not least, with the validation rules route, confusion, a negative user experience, and clutter in the page layout skyrockets if developers or architects are tasked with adding a few custom buttons or links to the page layout specific to the manufacturing industry!

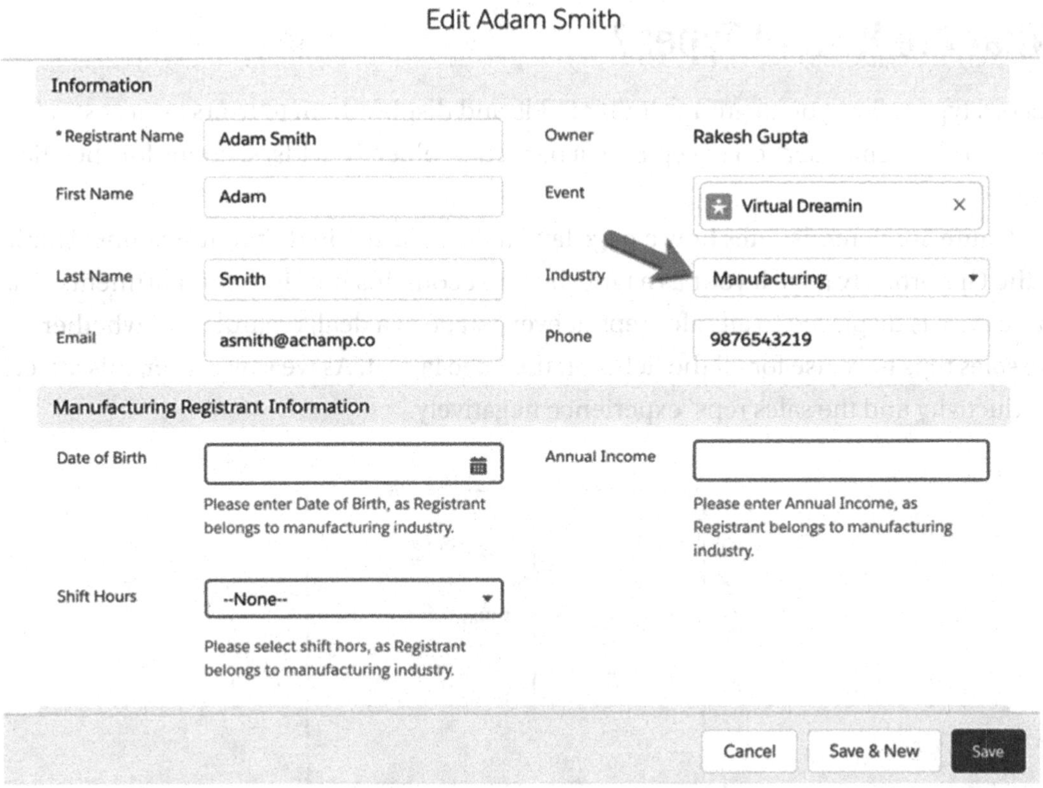

Figure 5-1. *Required fields based on the Industry drop-down*

Still not convinced the validation rules route may be a suboptimal solution? Well then, let us take a look at another example.

Assume the marketing director is happy with the validation rules solution you provided, and that it works as of today. However, the director now walks into your office and tasks you with a new requirement: she wants the value in the Industry field to be Shipping. When the value in the Industry field is Shipping, you need to create more than 40 fields. The marketing director also wants to gather additional data, such as participants' current job duties and bonuses, when the value is Shipping. To avoid confusion, a negative user experience, and clutter in the page layout, the director does not want the 40 fields to be displayed if the value in the Industry field is not Shipping.

In light of this situation, do you still think the validation rules route is an optimal solution? I don't think so either. To conclude, because page layout doesn't allow users to show/hide fields based on the value of another field, the validation rules route falls short. Developing a solution for the various scenarios just described requires developers and architects to use record types as an option.

What Are Record Types?

Record types allow you to group similar fields and display them to users as necessary. They do so by enabling you to segment a particular object's fields/sections for specific uses.

Figure 5-2 demonstrates how a page layout is organized in different sections. Think of the Opportunity page layout as a large box that contains multiple compartments. The same page is displayed to all sales reps at every stage of a deal, regardless of whether the sales reps have use for all the fields on the page layout. As we saw earlier, this affects productivity and the sales reps' experience negatively.

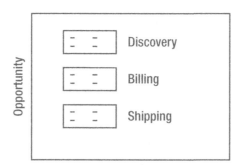

Figure 5-2. *A page layout is organized in different sections*

Record types to rescue! Record types help improve the sales rep experience by displaying appropriate sections/fields on a page layout based on an Opportunity stage. Record types are used mainly for two purposes:

1. To show different page layouts based on conditions. For example, if an Opportunity stage is Closed Won or Closed Lost, then, display the Read Only page layout.

2. To show/hide picklist values. For example, if an Opportunity type is Existing business, then remove the following values from the Lead Source field:

   - Partner

   - Employee Referral

   - Other

As a developer, you can create three different page layouts—Discovery, Billing, and Shipping—then display different fields on the page layout based on the value in the Opportunity stage field.

Table 5-2 represents the page layouts and their dependency based on the Opportunity stage. To control fields in page layouts based on the Opportunity stage, you need to use a record type.

Table 5-2. *Page Layouts and Their Dependency on the* Opportunity *Stage*

Page Layout	Stage
Discovery	Prospecting
Billing	Proposal/Price Quote
Shipping	Closed Won

Figure 5-3 demonstrates how record types control page layouts based on different stages. One record type can assign different page layouts to different profiles, or one record type can assign a single page layout to multiple profiles. In Figure 5-3, record type controls discovery page layouts 1 and 2 based on the profiles. So far so good. Let's take this discussion one level up.

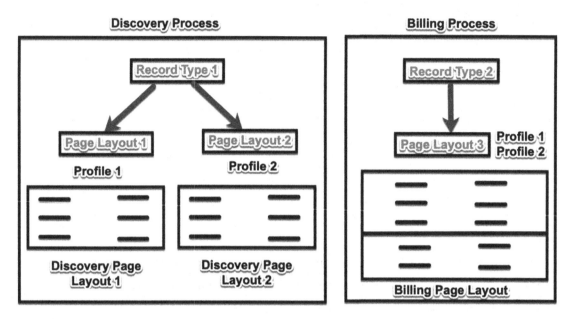

Figure 5-3. *Record types control page layouts*

Let's get back to our business scenario with Robin Guzman. He's received a request from his manager to configure the Registrant custom object based on Table 5-1.

He performs the following steps to meet this requirement using record types and page layouts:

1. Robin navigates to Setup (gear icon) ➤ Setup ➤ Object Manager ➤ Create ➤ Custom Object and creates a new custom object, Registrant, and all the fields mentioned in Table 5-1.

2. Next, he creates two page layouts by navigating to Setup (gear icon) ➤ Setup ➤ Object Manager ➤ Registrant ➤ Page Layouts.

The Registrant page layout should look like Figure 5-4.

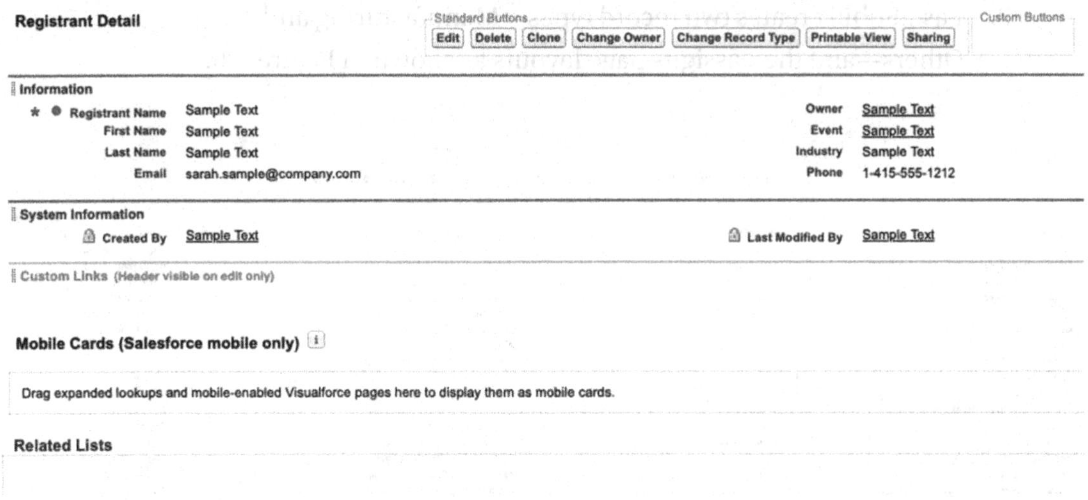

Registrant Detail

Standard Buttons

Edit Delete Clone Change Owner Change Record Type Printable View Sharing

Custom Buttons

Information

★ ● Registrant Name   Sample Text
    First Name   Sample Text
    Last Name   Sample Text
    Email   sarah.sample@company.com

Owner   Sample Text
Event   Sample Text
Industry   Sample Text
Phone   1-415-555-1212

System Information

🔒 Created By   Sample Text

🔒 Last Modified By   Sample Text

Custom Links (Header visible on edit only)

Mobile Cards (Salesforce mobile only) ⓘ

Drag expanded lookups and mobile-enabled Visualforce pages here to display them as mobile cards.

Related Lists

Figure 5-4. *Registrant page layout*

The Manufacturing Registrant page layout should look like Figure 5-5.

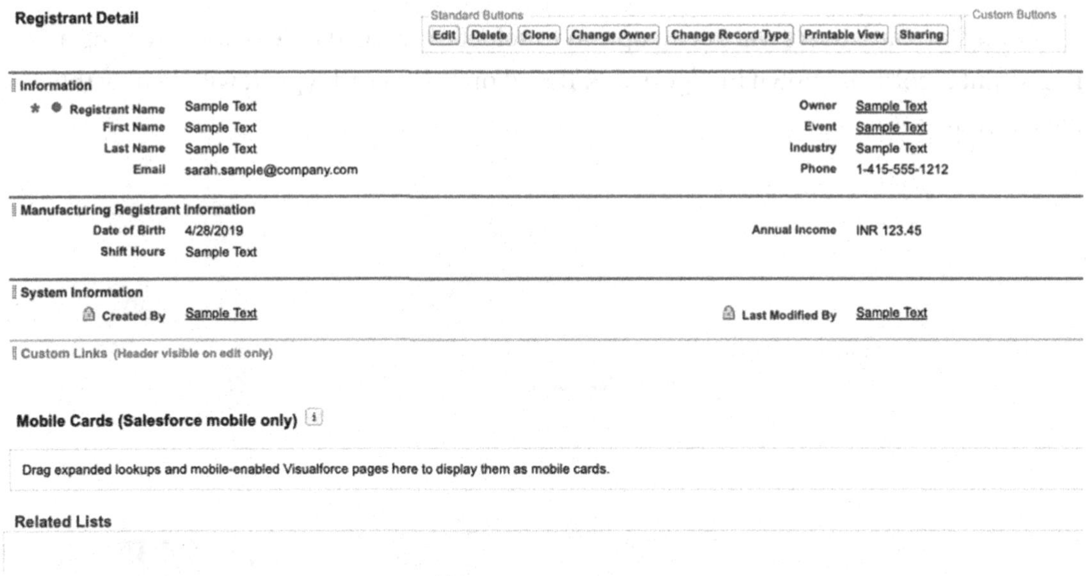

Registrant Detail

Standard Buttons

Edit Delete Clone Change Owner Change Record Type Printable View Sharing

Custom Buttons

Information

★ ● Registrant Name   Sample Text
    First Name   Sample Text
    Last Name   Sample Text
    Email   sarah.sample@company.com

Owner   Sample Text
Event   Sample Text
Industry   Sample Text
Phone   1-415-555-1212

Manufacturing Registrant Information

Date of Birth   4/28/2019
Shift Hours   Sample Text

Annual Income   INR 123.45

System Information

🔒 Created By   Sample Text

🔒 Last Modified By   Sample Text

Custom Links (Header visible on edit only)

Mobile Cards (Salesforce mobile only) ⓘ

Drag expanded lookups and mobile-enabled Visualforce pages here to display them as mobile cards.

Related Lists

Figure 5-5. *Registrant page layout for manufacturing*

3. Last, Robin creates two record types—Manufacturing and
    Others—and then assigns page layouts as shown in Figure 5-6.

| Save | Cancel |

Page Layout To Use: -- Select Page Layout --   ◆   0 Selected   0 Changed

| Profiles | Record Types | | (1-3 of 3) |
	Master	Manufacturing	Others
API User	Registrant Layout	Manufacturing Registrant Layout	Registrant Layout
Certification User	Registrant Layout	Manufacturing Registrant Layout	Registrant Layout
Chatter External User	Registrant Layout	Manufacturing Registrant Layout	Registrant Layout
Chatter Free User	Registrant Layout	Manufacturing Registrant Layout	Registrant Layout
Chatter Moderator User	Registrant Layout	Manufacturing Registrant Layout	Registrant Layout
Contract Manager	Registrant Layout	Manufacturing Registrant Layout	Registrant Layout
Finance User	Registrant Layout	Manufacturing Registrant Layout	Registrant Layout
General Marketing User	Registrant Layout	Manufacturing Registrant Layout	Registrant Layout
Instructor User	Registrant Layout	Manufacturing Registrant Layout	Registrant Layout
Marketing User	Registrant Layout	Manufacturing Registrant Layout	Registrant Layout
Professional Services Manager	Registrant Layout	Manufacturing Registrant Layout	Registrant Layout
Read Only	Registrant Layout	Manufacturing Registrant Layout	Registrant Layout
Sales User	Registrant Layout	Manufacturing Registrant Layout	Registrant Layout
Service Cloud	Registrant Layout	Manufacturing Registrant Layout	Registrant Layout
Solution Manager	Registrant Layout	Manufacturing Registrant Layout	Registrant Layout
Standard User	Registrant Layout	Manufacturing Registrant Layout	Registrant Layout
Support User	Registrant Layout	Manufacturing Registrant Layout	Registrant Layout
System Administrator	Registrant Layout	Manufacturing Registrant Layout	Registrant Layout
Training User	Registrant Layout	Manufacturing Registrant Layout	Registrant Layout

| Save | Cancel |

Figure 5-6. *Assigning page layouts based on record types and profiles*

Going forward, users will get an option to select the record type before creating a
Registrant record, as shown in Figure 5-7. Based on the record type, it will display the
page layout.

New Registrant

Select a record type

● Manufacturing

○ Others

| Cancel | Next |

Figure 5-7. *Option to select a record type*

How Record Types Control Lightning Record Pages

I have seen many questions from people, as part of the Trailblazer Community, wondering how record types and page layouts are connected in Lightning record pages. Here is my answer: a record type can control both page layout *and* Lightning record pages at the same time, because they are separate components.

Still confused on how record types control Lightning pages and page layouts? Well, let me show you an architectural diagram (Figure 5-8) that displays the connections among record types, Lightning record pages, and page layouts.

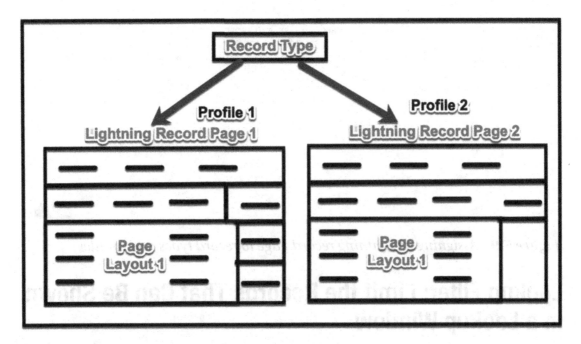

Figure 5-8. *How record type controls Lightning record pages and page layouts*

Figure 5-8 also shows that users in two different profiles can not only have the *same page layout*, but also they can have *different Lightning record pages* configured for their profiles—and vice versa!

Basically, in Lightning Experience, you use Classic page layout as a component (Record Detail), which sits on top of the Lightning record page. This means both are separate Lightning components. Therefore, both are configurable at the object level.

After you create a Lightning record page, click the Activation button to assign the Lightning record page based on record types and profiles.

Figure 5-9 demonstrates how you can assign a Lightning record page to record types and profiles in Lightning App Builder.

Figure 5-9. *Assigning a Lightning record page to record types and profiles*

Lookup Filter: Limit the Records That Can Be Shown in a Lookup Window

A lookup filter is one of the best tools to enrich data quality by enforcing data consistency. The filters limit fields and values displayed in a lookup dialog and, as a result, enforce access to valid values. The filter can be used when objects are in a lookup, master detail, or hierarchical relationship.

Let's look at an example. Pamela Kline has been given the requirement to restrict the Account Name field on opportunities by only allowing accounts with type Customer and by filtering out any other types of accounts.

To meet the requirement, Pamela performs the following steps:

1. She clicks Setup (gear icon) ➤ Setup ➤ Object Manager ➤ Opportunity ➤ Fields & Relationship ➤ Account Name and then clicks the Edit button.

2. Then, she navigates to the Lookup Filter section and clicks Show Filter Settings.

3. Pamela clicks the search icon and chooses Account Name. Then she chooses Type and clicks Insert.

4. For Operator, she chooses equals.

5. For Value/Field, she chooses Value.

6. Then, she clicks the search icon and chooses Customer.

7. Next, she clicks Insert Suggested Criteria.

8. At the end, she makes sure the filter type is set to Required and the Active check box is selected, as shown in Figure 5-10.

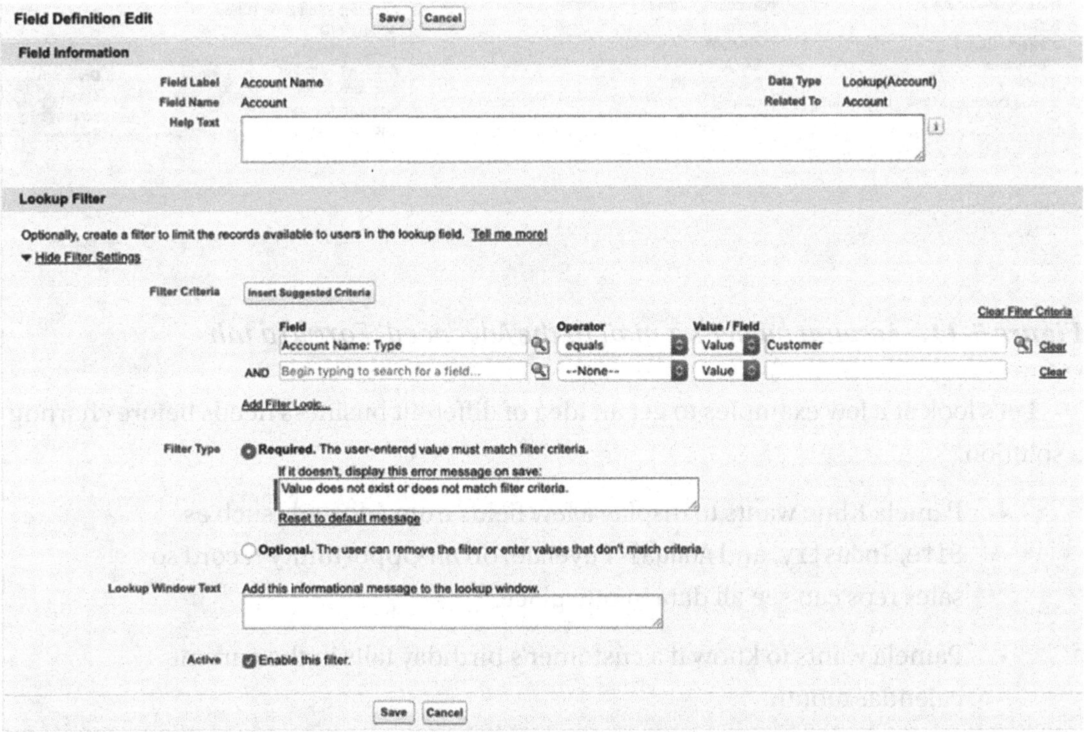

Figure 5-10. Configuration options available for the lookup filter

9.   When done, Pamela clicks the Save button.

Going forward, whenever a sales rep creates a new opportunity, Salesforce only shows the account's whose type is Customer.

Formula Fields: Small Work, Big Impact

Formula fields are Read Only fields that display values based on a formula's expression that you define. When writing a formula's expression, you can refer to fields from the parent object, and it can go ten levels deeper. This means, for example, when writing a formula on an Opportunity object, you can refer to the account owner's e-mail, as shown in Figure 5-11.

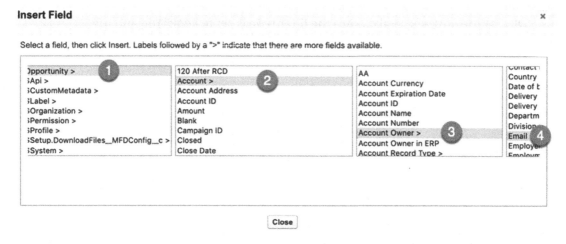

Figure 5-11. *Account owner's e-mail in the* Advanced Formula *tab*

Let's look at a few examples to get an idea of different business needs before charting a solution.

- Pamela Kline wants to display a few fields from Account, such as Site, Industry, and Annual Revenue, on an Opportunity record so sales reps can see all data in one place.

- Pamela wants to know if a customer's birthday falls in the current calendar month.

- Pamela wants to create a clickable phone number field that dials a phone number automatically, using a dialing tool, when clicked.

- Carolina Lopez, a sales manager at GoC, wants to share monthly installation with support agents, but not the Loan Amount and Interest Rate fields, which reside in the Loan Details custom object.

The common objective in all the aforementioned scenarios is to perform some kind of automation. There are a few automation tools in Salesforce and each one has unique features. For now, we will use formula fields to solve the business scenarios just presented. In the next chapter, however, we study several automation tools in depth.

When you reference a field from the parent object in a formula's expression, this type of formula is known as a *cross-object formula*, as shown in the screenshot in Figure 5-11. Using cross-object formulas, you can reference a field from the parent object (regardless of the whether the relationship is lookup or master detail).

You can create formula fields on standard or custom objects, but not on an external object. As of the Summer 2019 release, it is not possible to refer to fields on external objects in a formula. Any changes in the formula's expression are reflected automatically in the formula's field value.

Let's rejoin Pamela Kline, a system administrator at GoC, who has been given the requirement to display the annual revenue of a customer on the Contact record.

To meet the requirement, Pamela performs the following steps:

1. She clicks Setup (gear icon) ➤ Setup ➤ Object Manager ➤ Contact ➤ Fields & Relationship and clicks the New button.

2. Then she selects Formula as the data type and clicks the Next button.

3. She enters the field label Annual Revenue and chooses Currency as the data type, then clicks the Next button.

4. Pamela selects the Advanced Formula tab (1 in Figure 5-12) in the formula editor and then clicks Insert Field (2 in Figure 5-12). (The advanced formula editor contains many tools to create powerful formulas.)

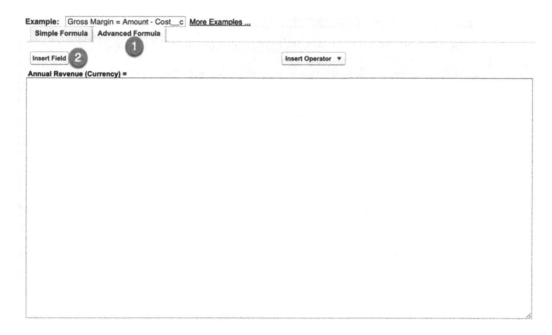

Figure 5-12. *Selecting the advanced formula editor*

5. Next, Pamela navigates to Contact (1 in Figure 5-13) ➤ Account
    (2 in Figure 5-13) ➤ Annual Revenue (3 in Figure 5-13) and clicks
    the Insert button (4 in Figure 5-13) to select the Annual Revenue
    field from the Account object.

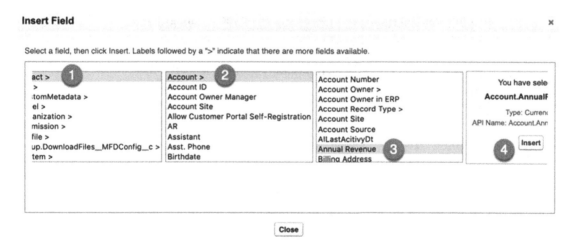

Figure 5-13. *Field selection in the formula editor*

6. When done, Pamela sees the formula's expression (1 in Figure 5-14) in the text area. She can also use the functions (2 in Figure 5-14) provided by Salesforce to write a complex formula. (Functions are convoluted operations that are preimplemented by Salesforce.) After Pamela writes the formula, she clicks the Check Syntax button (3 in Figure 5-14) to confirm everything is in working order before saving. If there is a problem with her formula, the syntax checker will warn her.

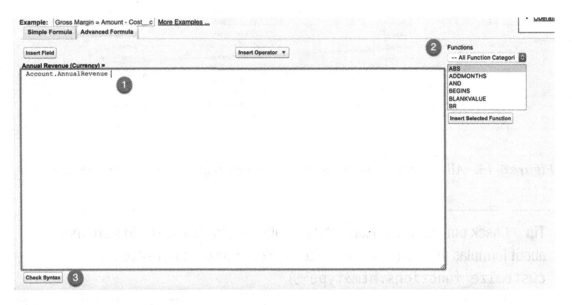

Figure 5-14. *Formula editor overview*

7. Pamela the clicks the Next button, which redirects her to the page where she can establish field-level security. She does not make any changes, but leaves all the settings as default settings.

8. She clicks the Next button again, which allows her to add the formula field to her page layout.

9. Once done, she clicks the Save button.

Salesforce populates values in the Annual Revenue field (which is a formula field) for all contacts in the Salesforce database. Remember, formula fields are Read Only fields and no one is allowed to edit their value. Formula fields can be used in list views to filter data, as shown in Figure 5-15.

	NAME ↑	ACCOUNT NAME	ANNUAL REVENUE	MAILING COUNTRY	
1	Amelia Rudnicki	Extensive Enterprise	USD 1,143,275,254.95	United Kingdom	▾
2	Andy Smith	Universal Technologies	USD 139,000,000.00	United States	▾
3	Antoinette Barone	Red Packages	USD 116,000,000.00	United States	▾
4	Arthur Sawyer	Alvarez Electrical	USD 169,000,000.00	United States	▾
5	Brent Anctil	Electric Company	USD 124,000,000.00	United States	▾
6	Brett Blake	St Francis Hospital	USD 134,000,000.00	United States	▾
7	Chris Clay	St Francis Hospital	USD 134,000,000.00	United States	▾
8	Curtis Maughlin	West Airlines	USD 198,000,000.00	United States	▾
9	Desiree Gonzalez	Buck Foods	USD 131,000,000.00	United States	▾
10	Evan Everson	Allen Brothers Labs	USD 117,000,000.00	United States	▾
11	Fletcher Dickerson	George Mobile	USD 165,000,000.00	United States	▾
12	Floyd Mathews	Mckinney Foods Corp	USD 139,000,000.00	United States	▾
13	Frank Frederick	Allen Brothers Labs	USD 117,000,000.00	United States	▾
14	Gianna Martinez	Galaxy Corp	USD 1,143,275,254.95	United Kingdom	▾
15	Jannis Morris	Thatherton Fuels	USD 500,000,000.00	Australia	▾
16	Jocelyn Archila	ABC Telecom	USD 762,183,503.30	United Kingdom	▾
17	Jon Airaudi	Berk Hath Inc	USD 174,000,000.00	United States	▾
18	Kevin Adams	West Airlines	USD 198,000,000.00	United States	▾
19	Lisa Hernandez	Barrytron	USD 1,000,000,000.00	Australia	▾
20	Marlene Molina	General Services Corporation	USD 2,000,000,000.00	Australia	▾
21	Michael Toy	LexCorp	USD 1,143,275,254.95	United Kingdom	▾
22	Ned Hardy	Mccormick Telecoms Corporation	USD 200,000,000.00	United States	▾
23	Nick Bartlett	Glenn Media	USD 160,000,000.00	United States	▾

Figure 5-15. *All customers whose annual revenue is greater than US$100,000,000*

Tip   Check out the help documentation published by Salesforce to learn more
about formulas (`https://help.salesforce.com/articleView?id=`
`customize_functions.htm&type=5`).

Rollup Summary Field

A rollup summary field is a custom field used to calculate values from related records
and to display the value on a parent record. You can create rollup summary fields on
parent records only if the objects have a master detail relationship.

For example, suppose there is a master detail relationship between the College
and Student custom objects, where College is the parent object and Student is a child
object. Using a rollup summary field, you can display the number of students currently
active for each college record, as shown in Figure 5-16.

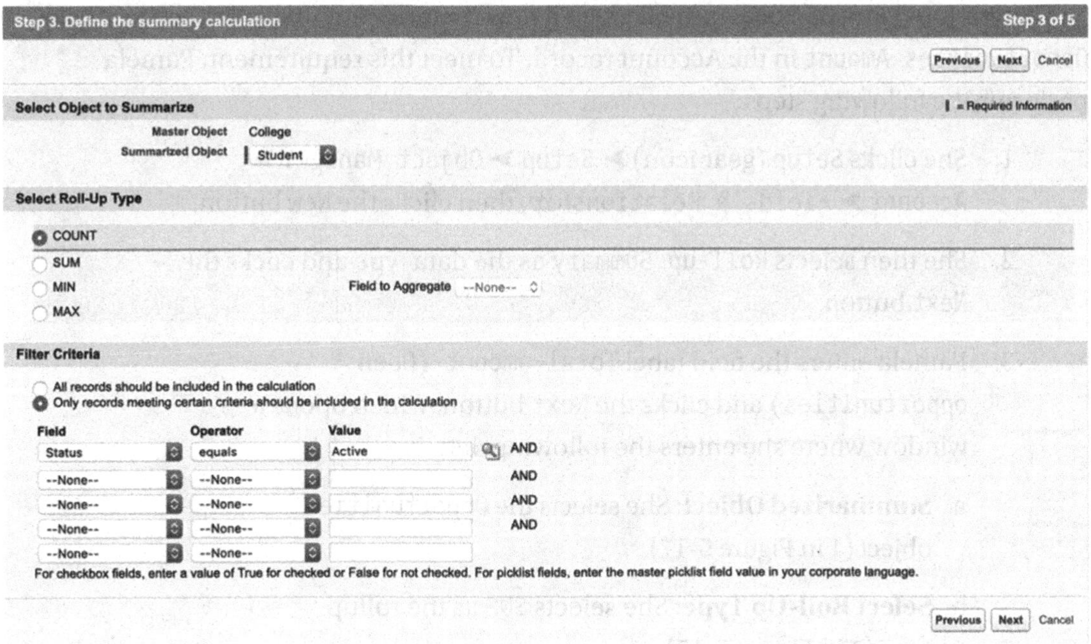

Figure 5-16. *Rollup summary field for the College record to determine the number of active students*

A rollup summary field contains different functions, such as the following:

- **COUNT**: This function is used to count the total number of related records.

- **SUM**: This function is used to sum values in the related record's field. You select the field from the `Field to Aggregate` drop-down. Only currency, number, and percent fields are available for selection.

- **MIN**: This function is used to find the minimum value on a field. You select the field from the `Field to Aggregate` drop-down, across all related records. Only currency, date, date/time, number, and percent fields are available for selection.

- **MAX**: This function is used to find the maximum value on a field. You select the field from the `Field to Aggregate` drop-down, across all related records. Only the currency, date, date/time, number, and percent fields are available for selection.

Let's rejoin Pamela. She has been given a new requirement to display Sum of Open Opportunities Amount in the Account record. To meet this requirement, Pamela performs the following steps:

1. She clicks Setup (gear icon) ➤ Setup ➤ Object Manager ➤ Account ➤ Fields & Relationship, then clicks the New button.

2. She then selects Roll-up Summary as the data type and clicks the Next button.

3. Pamela enters the field label Total amount (Open opportunities) and clicks the Next button, which opens a window where she enters the following details:

   a. **Summarized Object**: She selects the Opportunities object (1 in Figure 5-17).

   b. **Select Roll-Up Type:** She selects SUM as the rollup type (2 in Figure 5-17).

   c. **Field to Aggregate**: She selects Amount in the Field to Aggregate drop-down (3 in Figure 5-17).

   d. **Filter Criteria**: She selects Only records meeting certain criteria should be included in the calculation (3 in Figure 5-17) and then she selects Closed ➤ equals to False (4 in Figure 5-17) as filter criteria. At the end, her screen looks like Figure 5-17.

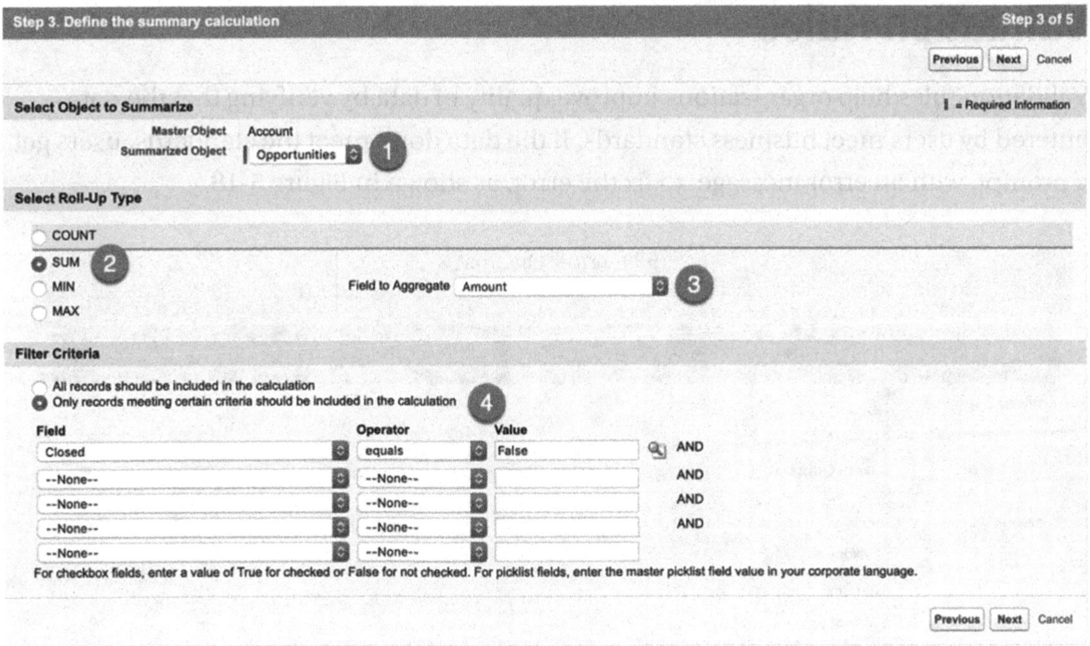

Figure 5-17. *Rollup summary field to summarize the open opportunities amount*

4.   When done, Pamela clicks the Next button, which redirects her to
     the page where she can establish field-level security. She doesn't
     make any changes, but leaves them as default values.

5.   She clicks the Next button, which allows her to add the rollup
     summary field to her page layout.

6.   Last, Pamela clicks the Save button.

Salesforce now populates Total amount (Open opportunities) field values for all
opportunities. Remember, rollup summary fields are Read Only fields; no one is allowed
to edit their value.

Tip   Check out the help documentation published by Salesforce to discover
hidden gems regarding the rollup summary field (https://help.salesforce.
com/articleView?id=fields_about_roll_up_summary_fields.
htm&type=s).

Validation Rules

Validation rules help organizations improve quality of data by verifying that the data entered by users meet business standards. If the data don't meet the standards, users get a prompt, with an error message, to fix the error, as shown in Figure 5-18.

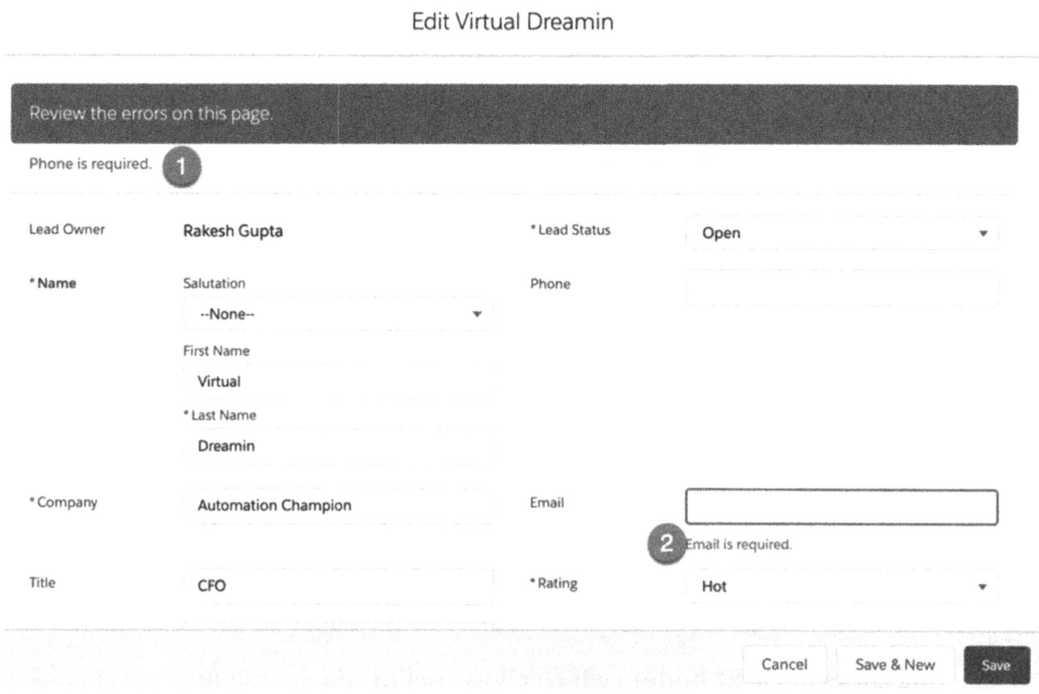

Figure 5-18. *Validation rules error messages*

A validation rule can contain a formula that evaluates the data in one or more fields and returns a value that is either True or False, where true means no error and false means there is an error. You can display the validation rule error message either at the top of the page (1 in Figure 5-18) or next to the field (2 in Figure 5-18).

Pamela Kline has been tasked with a requirement to validate that an account's annual revenue is not negative and does not exceed US$1,000,000,000. To meet the requirement, Pamela performs the following steps:

1.   She clicks Setup (gear icon) ➤ Setup ➤ Object Manager ➤ Account ➤ Validation Rules, then clicks the New button. This opens a window where she enters the following details:

a. **Rule Name**: Pamela types `Annual_revenue_cannt_be_greater_than_1bn`.

b. **Description**: She writes some meaningful text so other developers and administrators can understand easily why this custom field was created.

c. **Error Condition Formula**: She uses the following formula:

```
OR(
    AnnualRevenue < 0,
    AnnualRevenue > 1000000000
)
```

d. **Error Message**: She enters the following message: `Annual revenue cannot exceed 1 billion.`

e. **Error Location**: She selects the `Annual Revenue` field.

2. At the end, her screen looks like Figure 5-19.

Validation Rule Edit   Save   Save & New   Cancel

Rule Name | Annual_revenue_cannt_be_greater_than_1bn

Active   ☑

Description | Please refer JIRA request 215 for detailed requirement.

①

Error Condition Formula

Example: | Discount_Percent__c>0.30 | More Examples ...

Display an error if Discount is more than 30%

If this formula expression is **true**, display the text defined in the Error Message area

Functions

-- All Function Categori ⬍

ABS
ADDMONTHS
AND
BEGINS
BLANKVALUE
BR

[Insert Field]   [Insert Operator ▼]

```
OR(
AnnualRevenue < 0,
AnnualRevenue > 1000000000
)
```

Insert Selected Function

ABS(number)
Returns the absolute value of a
number, a number without its sign

Help on this function

[Check Syntax] No errors found

Error Message

Example: | Discount percent cannot exceed 30% |

This message will appear when Error Condition formula is **true**

Error Message | Annual Revenue cannot exceed 1 billion.

This error message can either appear at the top of the page or below a specific field on the page

Error Location | ○ Top of Page ◉ Field   Annual Revenue   ⬍ ⓘ

Save   Save & New   Cancel

Figure 5-19. *A validation rule to check annual revenue*

3. Last, Pamela clicks the Save button.

Going forward, if users update their annual revenue with an amount greater than US$1,000,000,000, they get an error message and have to fix the error before they can save the record.

Tip   Check out the help documentation published by Salesforce to find examples of validation rules (`https://help.salesforce.com/articleView?id=fields_useful_field_validation_formulas.htm&type=5`).

Custom Permissions: A Way to Bypass Validation Rules

Pamela is very happy. She just got an appreciation e-mail from her manager for all the work she has done, but it's then followed by another request: is it possible to bypass the annual revenue validation rule for the following users, for now?

- Carolina Lopez, Regional Sales Manager

- Jerry Shannon, VP Sales

- Donna Serdula, Senior Vice President

Pamela is also told that, in the future, the list of users may grow!

Fortunately, Pamela knows how to bypass validation rules for specific users or profiles. For example, she can bypass the annual revenue validation rule for system administrators by adding a condition to check their profile, as shown in Figure 5-20.

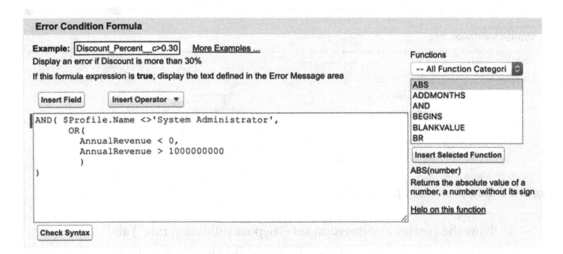

Figure 5-20. *Bypass a validation rule for a system administrator's profile*

Pamela wonders whether there is a better way to handle this requirement. She doesn't want to modify the validation rule every time she is required to add a new user to the bypass validation list.

Custom permissions to rescue! Pamela learned recently that, by using custom permissions, she can grant users access to custom apps. In Salesforce, she can use custom permissions to check which users can access a certain functionality. Using custom permissions, she can bypass validation rules, formula fields, Process Builder, Apex triggers, and so on. Custom permissions let her define access checks that can be assigned to users via profiles or permission sets.

To meet the requirement, Pamela performs the following steps:

1. She clicks Setup (gear icon) ➤ Setup ➤ PLATFORM TOOLS ➤ Custom Code ➤ Custom Permissions, and clicks the New button.

2. She creates a custom permission, as shown in Figure 5-21.

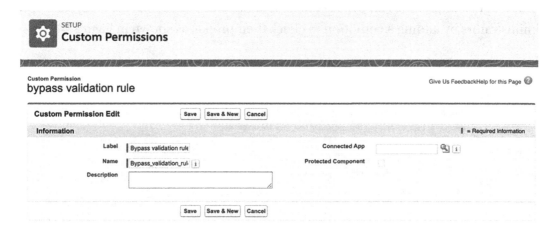

Figure 5-21. *A custom permission*

3. Now she creates a permission set ("Bypass validation rule") and assigns the custom permission Bypass Validation Rule to it, as shown in Figure 5-22).

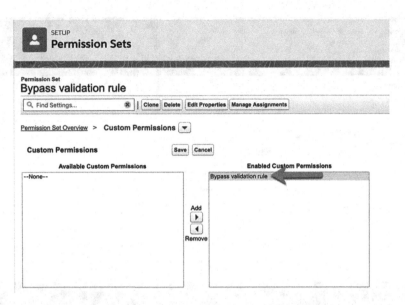

Figure 5-22. *Assigning custom permission to a permission set*

4. Next, Pamela modifies the annual revenue validation rule to add a custom permission check. To do so, she navigates to Setup (gear icon) ➤ Setup ➤ Object Manager ➤ Account ➤ Validation Rules and edits the annual revenue validation rule.

5. She modifies the formula as follows:

```
AND(NOT($Permission.Bypass_validation_rule), OR(
      AnnualRevenue < 0,
      AnnualRevenue > 1000000000
      )
)
```

6. To select the custom permission, she clicks Insert Field (1 in Figure 5-23) and then $Permission ➤ Bypass_validation_rule ➤ Insert (2 in Figure 5-23).

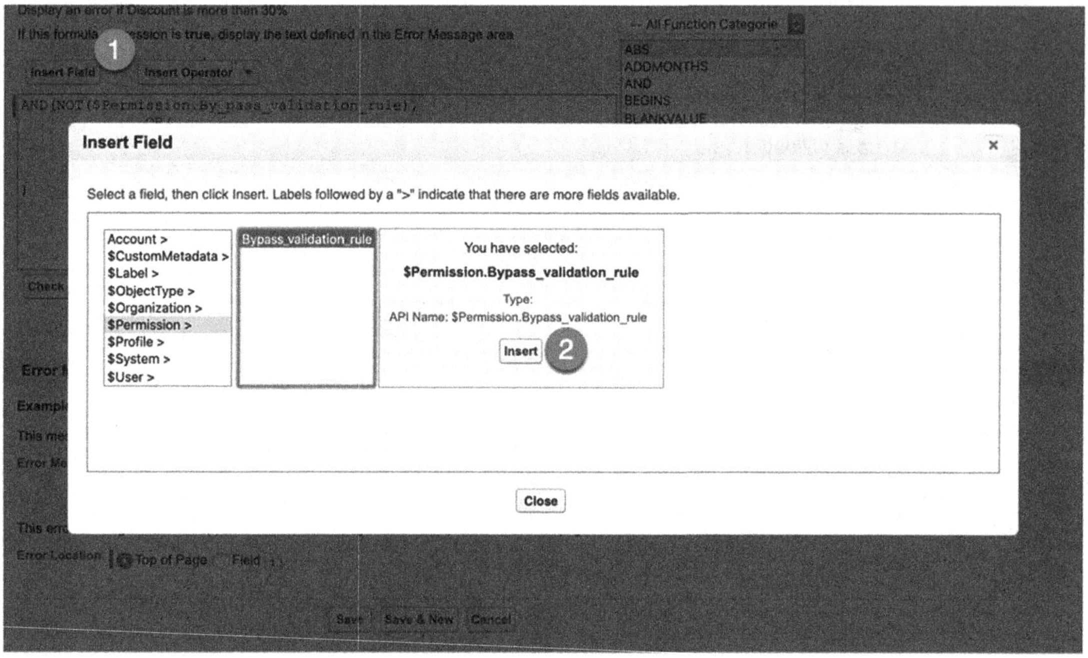

Figure 5-23. *Selecting a custom permission*

7. Last, she clicks the Save button.

Pamela assigns the Bypass Validation Rule permission to users Carolina Lopez, Jerry Shannon, and Donna Serdula. And that's it! Now the validation rule is bypassed for these users. In the future, if Pamela wants to bypass a validation rule for other users, all she has to do is to assign the permission set to those users.

Points to Remember

1. The following picklist fields are not available for record types because they are controlled by sales processes, lead processes, support processes, and solution processes respectively:

   a. Opportunity Stage

   b. Case Status

   c. Solution Status

   d. Lead Status

2. The following campaign member picklist fields are not available for record types:

    a. `Status`

    b. `Salutation`

    c. `Lead Source`

3. It is not possible to deactivate a record type if it is in use by the `Email-to-Case` or `On-Demand Email-to-Case` routing e-mail address.

4. Lookup filters improve user efficiency by controlling the number of available records in a lookup search dialog.

5. In Lightning Experience, a lookup filter doesn't work if a field referenced in the filtered lookup isn't added to the page layout.

6. It is not possible to refer to cross-object formulas in rollup summary fields.

7. Salesforce allows a maximum of ten unique relationships per object in cross-object formulas.

8. Formula fields can comprise up to 3900 characters, including spaces, return characters, and comments. If your formula needs more characters, create separate formula fields and reference them in another formula field.

9. It is not possible to reference long text areas, encrypted fields, or description fields in formulas.

10. It is not possible to delete fields referenced in formulas. Remove the field from the formula before deleting it.

11. When you delete a child record from a rollup summary field, Salesforce *does not recalculate the value of the field*. Select the `Force a mass recalculation` option on the edit page of the rollup summary field to recalculate the value manually.

12. When one validation rule fails, Salesforce continues to check other validation rules on that field, or other fields, on the page and displays all error messages at once.

13. It is possible to use rollup summary fields in validation rules. However, one *cannot use a rollup summary field as a location to display an error message*, because *rollup summary fields do not display on edit pages.*

14. You can create custom permissions only in the Enterprise edition or higher.

Hands-on Exercises

The following exercises will give you more practice with the platform, which ultimately will help you in gaining mastery of it, and also will assist you in preparing for the certification examination. Remember, these are hands-on exercises, and you can find the answers at the back of the book in the Appendix, but try to implement them in your Salesforce org, which is the primary goal of doing them.

1. Configure business processes on Lead in such a way that, when users create a lead for North America or Asia Pacific, they only see the following values on lead status:

   a. Lead status for North America

      New
      Suspect
      Interested
      Working
      Qualified (Converted)

   b. Lead status on Asia Pacific

      New

      Open

      Qualified (Converted)

2. Configure the Lead Lightning record page to include the following components:

   a. Activities

   b. Chatter

c. Related List Quick Links

Assign them to the North America record type only.

3. Dennis Williams, a system administrator at GoC, has to meet the following requirements for the Account Name field on the Contact object:

   a. The account name lookup dialog should only display accounts that have Mumbai as the site name.

   b. The previous constraint should not apply to users with a system administrator profile.

   How would you instruct Dennis to meet these requirements?

4. Business managers at GoC found that sales reps are creating opportunities for competitors' accounts. As an app builder, how can you restrict sales reps from selecting competitors' accounts while creating a new opportunity?

5. Create a custom field (data type: Lookup Relationship) on the Opportunity object with the Contact object. This should allow users to select a contact when creating a new opportunity.

6. Keeping the previous requirement in mind, configure the lookup in such a way that it only displays the contacts related to the account with which the opportunity is associated!

7. Dennis wants to implement opportunity management at GoC, but he is a bit confused by one of the requirements. Because you now have a better understanding of record sharing, please help him select the appropriate sharing architecture to fulfill the following requirements:

   a. When the opportunity amount is greater than US$1,000,000 make sure the Next Step field is required.

   b. However, make sure it doesn't apply to the following users:

      • Jerry Shannon, VP Sales

      • Users with a system administrator profile

      • Users with the sales rep-APAC profile

141

8. Help Dennis to write the correct formula for the following requirements (formula field):

    a. Create a custom field that determines the telephone country code of a contact based on the shipping country on the shipping address.

    b. Create a custom drop-down on a contact's preferred phone with the values Home Phone, Asst. Phone, Other Phone, and Phone. Now create a formula field that shows the phone number based on what the user provided in the Preferred Phone field.

    c. Create a formula field that displays the first three characters of a name and year from the Date of Birth field separated by a dash.

    d. Create a formula field on Account that displays the ratings Hot, Warm, or Cold based on the following criteria:

       • Annual revenue should be greater than US$50,000,000.

       • The billing country should contain United States, US, USA, CANADA, CA, MEXICO, MX .

       Now, if the account fulfills these two requirements and they belong to

       • type Reseller, Integrator, or Partner, then the rating should be Hot

       • type Prospect or Investor, then the rating should be Warm

       • everything else, then the rating should be Cold

    e. Create a formula field on the Opportunity object to calculate the number of days since an opportunity with an account was opened. If the opportunity is closed (either won or lost), this field should be blank.

    f. Create a formula field on the Contact object that displays the month as a text string instead of a number from the Date of Birth field.

    g. Create a formula field on Lead to calculate the number of days the lead has been open. If the lead is qualified or unqualified, then the formula field should be blank.

9. Help Dennis to write the correct formula for the following requirements (validation rule):

    a. Create a validation rule to prompt an error message to users if a quote line-item discount exceeds 23%.

    b. If the Phone field on the Contact object doesn't contain ten digits, display an error message to the users.

    c. Create the custom field Delivery Date on the Opportunity object. Now write a validation rule to make sure that this custom field must be populated if an opportunity stage is Closed Won or Negotiation/Review.

    d. Write a validation rule to make sure the close date of an opportunity cannot be in the past.

    e. Write a validation rule to make sure that users are only allowed to update the opportunity if they have added products to the opportunity.

    f. Write a validation rule that prevents sales reps from changing Opportunity Stage to anything other than Closed Won or Closed Lost, after Opportunity Stage is set to Closed Won or Closed Lost.

    g. Write a validation rule to make sure the probability of a lost opportunity is set to 0%.

10. Create a custom field on Account to display the maximum amount from the related opportunity that is marked Closed Won.

Summary

In this chapter, we covered record types and how they include pages in Salesforce Classic vs. Lightning Experience. We also studied different mechanisms to improve data quality using filter lookups and validation rules. Furthermore, we reviewed rollup summary and formula fields by examining a few examples. In the next chapter, we dive into how to automate business processes using out-of-the-box automation tools.

CHAPTER 6

Automating Business Processes

In Chapter 5, we covered record types, followed by an in-depth overview of data improvement tools such as lookup filters, formula fields, and rollup summary fields. Last, we looked at validation rules with real-life examples.

This chapter is comprised of three parts. Part one is divided into three sections, part two is divided into two sections, and part three consists of one section.

In part one, the first section includes of an overview of the Lightning Flow life cycle. The second section takes a close look at Lightning Flow Designer. A few use cases are discussed in the third section.

In part two, the first section consists of an overview of Lightning Process Builder, including when to use which automation tool. In the second section, we work through a few use cases of Lightning Process Builder.

In part three, we focus exclusively on the approval process, with a real-life example.

Introduction to Lightning Flow

Lightning Flow is a drag-and-drop interface that allows you to automate business processes by using clicks, not code. Using Lightning Flow, you can undertake a few actions; create, update, and delete records; send e-mail; submit records for approval; send notifications to Salesforce mobile; automate Quip; post a message to chatter; and, last but not least, create a guided process and make it available to end users.

Lightning Flow can run automatically without using any manual intervention. It has the ability to interact with Salesforce objects (many of them are not available through workflow rules or Lightning Process Builder) and to invoke Apex classes (an Apex class implements the `Process.Plugin` interface or `@InvocableMethod` annotation). Using

145

© Rakesh Gupta 2020
R. Gupta, *Salesforce Platform App Builder Certification*, https://doi.org/10.1007/978-1-4842-5479-0_6

Lightning Flow, you can create a series of screens to take user input to collect the data and process them in Salesforce, based on your logic.

Let's meet up with Pamela Kline again, who has just received a new request from her manager: add new users automatically to a public group named Company Announcements.

Pamela has several options for meeting this requirement:

1. **Apex trigger**: This option requires Apex programming skills. That said, Pamela must write a test class to deploy the Apex trigger into production, which is a time-consuming undertaking, to say the least.

```
trigger addintoPublicgroup on User (after insert) {
  for (User AddUser: trigger.new)
   {
               If (AddUser.Isactive == True)
         {
      // Your logic;
}
     }
     }
```

2. **Lightning Flow and Lightning Process Builder**: This option combines tools, as shown in Figure 6-1.

   a. In Lightning Flow, Pamela would write the logic to add people to the public group.

   b. Using Lightning Process Builder, Pamela can fire Lightning Flow whenever a user record gets created.

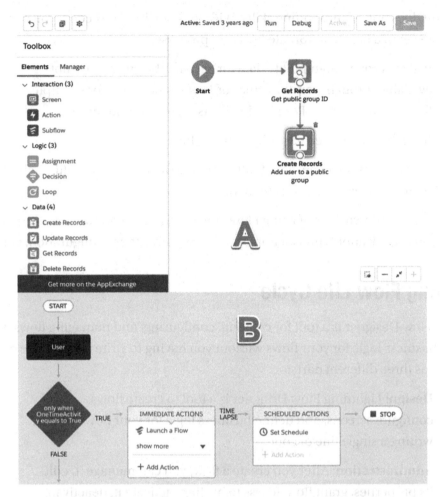

Figure 6-1. *A Lightning Flow and Lightning Process Builder solution*

Note   A flow can be fired automatically using Process Builder or, if it is scheduled to run at a specified time, it can run at a scheduled time.

Advantages of Using Lightning Flow

The benefits of using Lightning Flow over Apex include the following:

- The flow allows you to automate a business process using clicks, not code.

- It does not require coding skills. Without knowing Apex code, you can develop a flow to automate business processes.

- It allows you to manipulate data for certain objects that are not available through workflow rules or Process Builder—for example, Group, GroupMember, PermissionSetAssignment, and more.

- It can be maintained easily by nondevelopers.

- Because it is not code, you don't need to write test classes (although there are a few exceptions to this).

One of the few downsides of using Flow, however, is that you can make changes directly in an organization's production org, just like any other configuration. Ouch!

Lightning Flow Life Cycle

Lightning Flow Designer is a tool for creating, configuring, and managing flows. It is used to define business logic for your flows without you having to write a single line of code. Designer has three different parts:

1. **Design**: Lightning Flow Designer is a tool to create flows, configure screens, and define business logic for your flows without writing a single line of code.

2. **Administration**: After you create a flow, you can manage it, edit its properties, grant flow access to profiles, activate it, deactivate it, delete it, save it as a new version or a new flow, or just run an existing flow.

3. **Runtime**: You can run an active flow from a custom button, link, Flow action, Lightning page, and more. If it is an autolaunched flow, then it can be executed through Process Builder or run at a specified time.

An Overview of Lightning Flow Designer

As mentioned, Lightning Flow Designer is a tool to create flows, configure screens, and define business logic for your flows without requiring a single line of code. Flow Designer's user interface has several different functional parts (Figure 6-2):

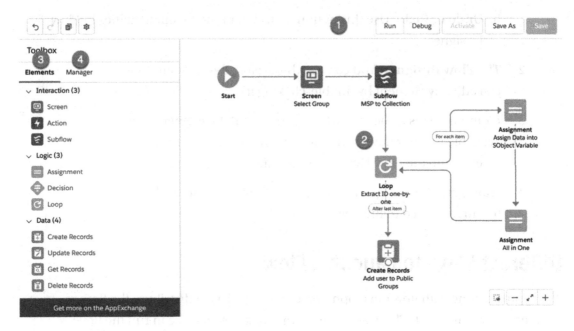

Figure 6-2. *Lightning Flow Designer*

1. **The button bar**: You can use the Save, Save As, Activate, Debug, Run, Undo, and Redo buttons to perform specific activities:

   a. **Save**: Use this option to save your flow.

   b. **Save As**: Use this option to clone a flow or create a new version of the flow

   c. **Activate**: Use this option to activate the flow.

   d. **Debug**: Use this option to see the real-time details of what your flow does and why it is not working. Set input variables and restart the flow at any time to debug a different branch.

   e. **Run**: Use this option to run the most recent version of the flow you are working on.

   f. **Flow Properties**: Click the screwdriver icon to see information related to your flow, such as name, unique name, description, flow type, interview label, version, and created and modified dates.

   g. **Copy** or **Paste**: Use this option to copy and paste a flow element (such as Screen, Create Records, and Decision) one at a time.

    h. **Undo** or **Redo**: Use this option to undo or redo recent activities in Flow Designer.

2. **The Flow Designer**: You can use this area to design your flow. You can edit any element by double-clicking it.

3. **Elements**: This is the area where you find all the element types available for your flow. You drag and drop elements from the palette onto the Flow Designer to use them.

4. **Manager**: The `Manager` tab contains all the elements and resources added to the flow.

Different Ways to Launch a Flow

After you are done with flow development, the next task is to distribute the flow so business users can use it. There are several ways business users can run the flow:

1. Flow Action

2. Lightning app page

3. Lightning home page

4. Custom button or link

5. Login flow

6. Process Builder

7. Automatically at a specified time

8. Lightning component

9. The Apex `start` () method

10. Visualforce page

This list is not exhaustive. Now that we've looked at the nuts and bolts of Lightning Flow, let's see how we can use it in real life.

Use Case 1: Mortgage Broker Commission Calculator

At GoC, mortgage brokers often get confused about their commission for a given deal. They are having a hard time calculating the commission correctly. Pamela Kline wants to create an application that allows mortgage brokers to calculate their commission.

On the very first screen, she wants to allow mortgage brokers to enter the property the value (in dollars) and the commission (as a percentage), as shown in Figure 6-3.

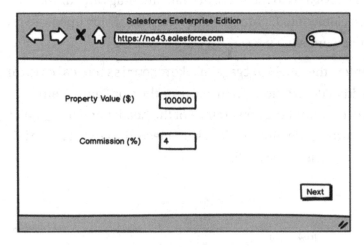

Figure 6-3. *Mortgage broker commission calculator*

On the next screen, Pamela wants to display the commission amount (in dollars), as shown in Figure 6-4.

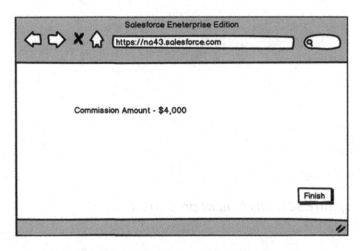

Figure 6-4. *Calculator displays the commission amount*

Pamela does this by performing the following steps:

1. She navigates to Setup (gear icon) ➤ Setup ➤ PLATFORM TOOLS ➤ Process Automation ➤ Flow.

2. She then clicks the New Flow button, which opens a pop-up, where she selects the Screen Flow option and then clicks the Create button. These actions open Lightning Flow Designer.

3. Pamela navigates to the Elements tab and drags and drops the Screen element to Lightning Flow Designer, which opens a Screen element window.

4. She enters the label Mortgage broker commission calculator and adds a description. Then she uses the Configure Frame section to control the appearance of the header and footer. Within the Control Navigation section, she selects the Next or Finish option only, as shown in Figure 6-5.

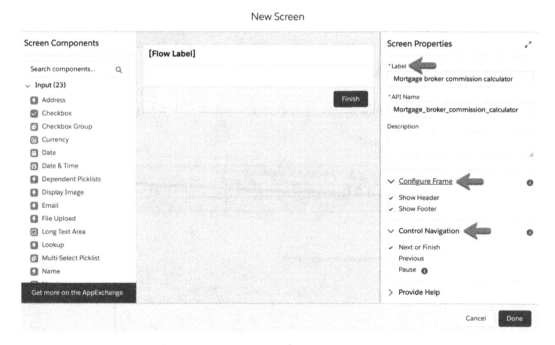

Figure 6-5. *Configure* Screen *element properties*

5. Next, Pamela uses the `Screen` element to display the fields so that mortgage brokers can enter the property value and their commission as a percentage. She drags and drops the `Currency` field onto the `Screen` element and configures it by clicking the `Currency` field to configure its settings by entering the following information:

   a. **Label**: She enters the label for the input currency field. In this case, Pamela enters `Property value ($)` as the label.

   b. **API Name**: This field autopopulates based on the label.

   c. **Require**: She selects this check box to make the field required.

   d. **Default Value**: Users can enter a default value for this field that would prepopulate the value for the component. For this requirement, Pamela leaves the field empty.

   e. **Decimal Places**: Pamela uses this field to control the number of digits to the right of the decimal point. She knows the number of digits can't exceed 17.

   f. **Set Component Visibility**: Pamela uses this section to control component visibility based on the flow's attributes.

   g. **Validate Input**: Here, Pamela knows she can provide a formula that evaluates whether the value that is entered is valid. She also knows she should add an error message to display if the value input is invalid.

   h. **Provide Help**: Pamela knows she can use this field to give her users more context with this screen component.

At the end, Pamela's screen component looks like Figure 6-6.

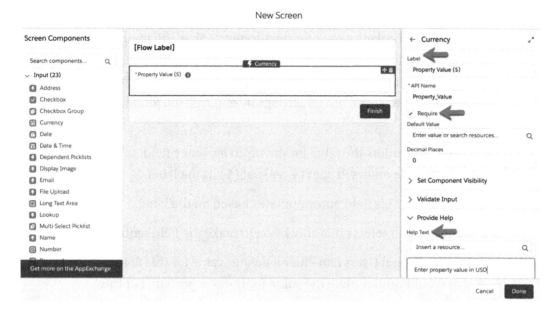

Figure 6-6. *Configure currency component properties*

6. Then, Pamela adds the Number field to allow mortgage brokers to
    enter their commission as a percentage. At the end, her flow looks
    like Figure 6-7.

Figure 6-7. *Configuring number component properties*

7. When she is finished, she clicks the Done button.

8. To calculate the commission amount, Pamela creates a formula. To do this, she navigates to the Manager tab and clicks the New Resource button. This opens a pop-up window where she configures the formula, as shown in Figure 6-8.

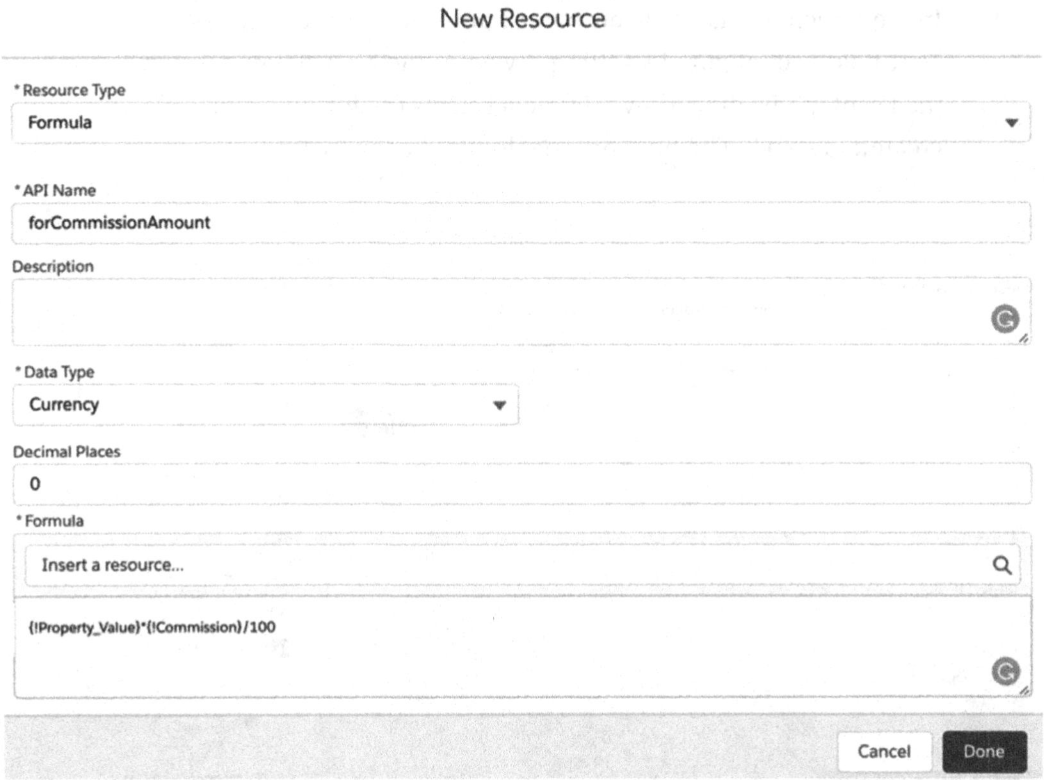

New Resource

* Resource Type

Formula ▼

* API Name

forCommissionAmount

Description

⟳

* Data Type

Currency ▼

Decimal Places

0

* Formula

Insert a resource... 🔍

{!Property_Value}*{!Commission}/100

⟳

Cancel   Done

Figure 6-8. Formula to calculate commission amount

{!Property_value} and {!Commission} are screen input fields Pamela created in steps 5 and 6.

9. When she is finished, she clicks the Done button.

10. The next task is for her to display the commission amount on the screen. For that, Pamela drags and drops the Screen element from Elements to Flow Designer. This opens a Screen element window, where Pamela enters the name Display mortgage commission

amount. She uses the Configure Frame section to control the appearance of the header and footer. Within the Control Navigation section, Pamela selects the Next or Finish option only.

11. Now she navigates to the Screen Component section and double-clicks Display Text, which is available in the Display section.

12. In the screen overlay preview pane, Pamela clicks the Display Text field to configure its settings by entering the API name. From the Display Text drop-down, Pamela selects the formula she created in step 8. The final product looks like Figure 6-9.

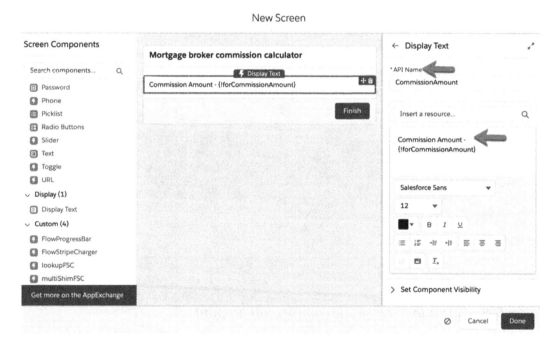

Figure 6-9. *Configure second screen to display commission amount*

13. When she is finished, Pamela clicks the Done button.

Connecting the Flow Elements

So far, Pamela has created two screens: one for getting the inputs from the mortgage broker and the other to display the commission amount in dollars. Now Pamela needs to connect both elements so that, at runtime, the flow can decide the order of execution of the elements.

1. To do this, in the Start element, Pamela finds the node at the bottom and drags the node to the target element, as shown in Figure 6-10.

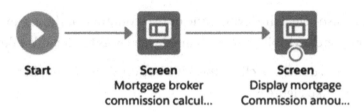

Figure 6-10. Connecting the flow elements

2. Next. Pamela she clicks the Save button and enters Mortgage broker commission calculator as the name to save the flow.

3. Pamela does not forget to activate the flow! She does so by clicking the Activate button.

Activating a Version of a Flow

When users activate a flow, Salesforce does not allow them to modify the activated flow. At this point, users have two options:

1. Create a new flow by cloning the activated flow.

2. Modify the activated flow, save it as a new version, and then modify it. When users are done with modification, they can activate the new version of the flow.

Users can have multiple versions of a flow, but they can activate only one version of a flow at a time. From the flow detail page, Salesforce allows users to activate or deactivate one version of a flow. Users click the Activate link next to the version of the flow they want.

Displaying a Flow from the Lightning Home Page

At this point, Pamela has created and activated a flow. The next step is to distribute it, so that mortgage brokers can use it. She wants to place this application on the Lightning home page. She does this by performing the following steps:

1. She edits the Lightning home page by navigating to App Builder.

2. She drags and drops the flow component onto the page.

3. Next, she selects the flow she wants to display—in this case, Mortgage Broker Commission Calculator.

4. She can also select the layout (one or two columns) and she can set component visibility, which Pamela leaves as the default value.

5. When she is done, she clicks the Save button. At then end, her flow looks like Figure 6-11.

I hope you now have a better understanding of how to create a flow and activate it for business users.

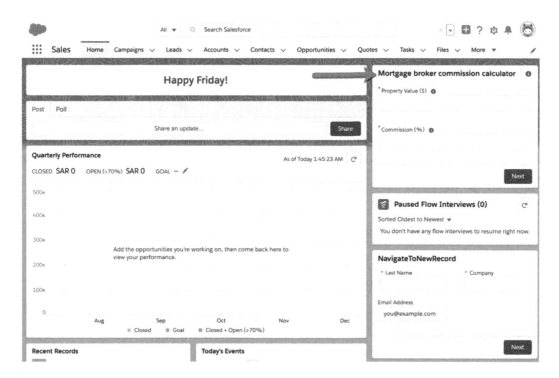

Figure 6-11. *Displaying a flow in the Lightning home page*

Use Case 2: Delete Unqualified Leads

Pamela Kline has received the following requirement from her manager: whenever a lead is updated as unqualified, delete it. This will help GoC maintain a clean database.

First, we have to understand why we need to use Lightning Flow here. Can't this be done through Process Builder? The answer is *no*! This is because, as of the proposed Winter 2020 release, a process built in Process Builder won't have the ability to *delete a record*.

A flow can be invoked manually using buttons, links, or actions. In Pamela's situation, she needs to call the flow automatically whenever a lead is updated to unqualified, and then delete the record. In such cases, we need to invoke the flow from Process Builder. Figure 6-12 shows the process flow diagram for the new business requirement.

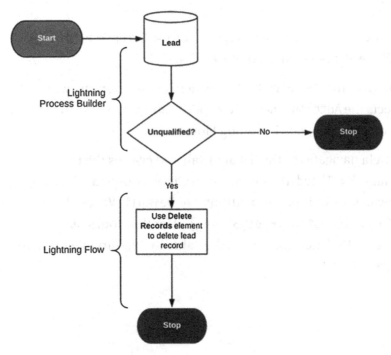

Figure 6-12. *Process flow diagram for use case 2*

Now that you understand why we need to use two tools to solve this requirement, let's plow through the following steps:

1. **Lightning Process Builder**: When a lead is updated as unqualified, Process Builder calls a flow and passes LeadId to it.

2. **Lightning Flow**: A flow is used to delete the Lead record based on the ID passed by Process Builder using the Delete Records element.

In this section, we look at Lightning Flow only. We look at the Process Builder part in the next section.

Pamela performs the following steps to solve the preceding business requirement using Lightning Flow:

1. She makes sure to add Unqualified as a value in the Lead Status field.

2. Then she navigates to Setup (gear icon) ➤ Setup ➤ PLATFORM TOOLS ➤ Process Automation ➤ Flow.

3. She clicks the New Flow button, which opens a pop-up, where she selects the Autolaunched Flow option, and then clicks the Create button, which opens Lightning Flow.

4. Pamela navigates to the Manager tab and creates the text variable VarTLeadID. She sets its availability outside the flow as available for input and output. For Default Value she uses {!$GlobalConstant.EmptyString}. Her flow looks like Figure 6-13. Later, she passes the value to this variable through Process Builder.

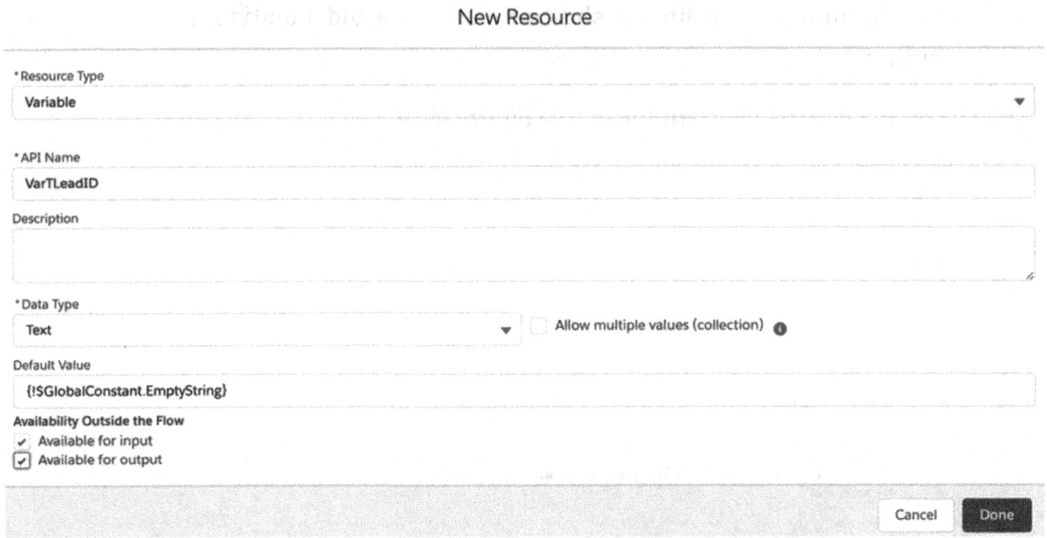

New Resource

* Resource Type

Variable ▼

* API Name

VarTLeadID

Description

* Data Type

Text ▼   ☐ Allow multiple values (collection) ⓘ

Default Value

{!$GlobalConstant.EmptyString}

Availability Outside the Flow
☑ Available for input
☑ Available for output

Cancel   Done

Figure 6-13. *Creating a text variable*

5. Pamela navigates to the Elements tab and drags and drops the Delete Records element onto Lightning Flow Designer. This opens a new window, where she enters the following details:

   a. **Label**: She enters the label for the input currency field. In this case, she enters Delete lead records as the label.

   b. **API Name**: This field autopopulates based on the label.

   c. **Description**: Pamela writes some meaningful text so other developers and administrators can understand easily why this Delete Records element was created. When users select the Delete Records element in the Explorer tab, the description appears in the Description area.

   d. **How to Find Records to Delete**: Pamela selects the Specify conditions option.

   e. **Delete Records of This Object Type**: She selects the object for which she wants to delete the record. In this case, she selects the Lead object.

6. Next, Pamela needs to set the filter criteria to identify which record gets deleted. In this scenario, she selects the Id = {!VarTLeadID} text variable.

7. To add multiple conditions, she could click the `Add Condition` button.

The `Delete Records` element looks like Figure 6-14.

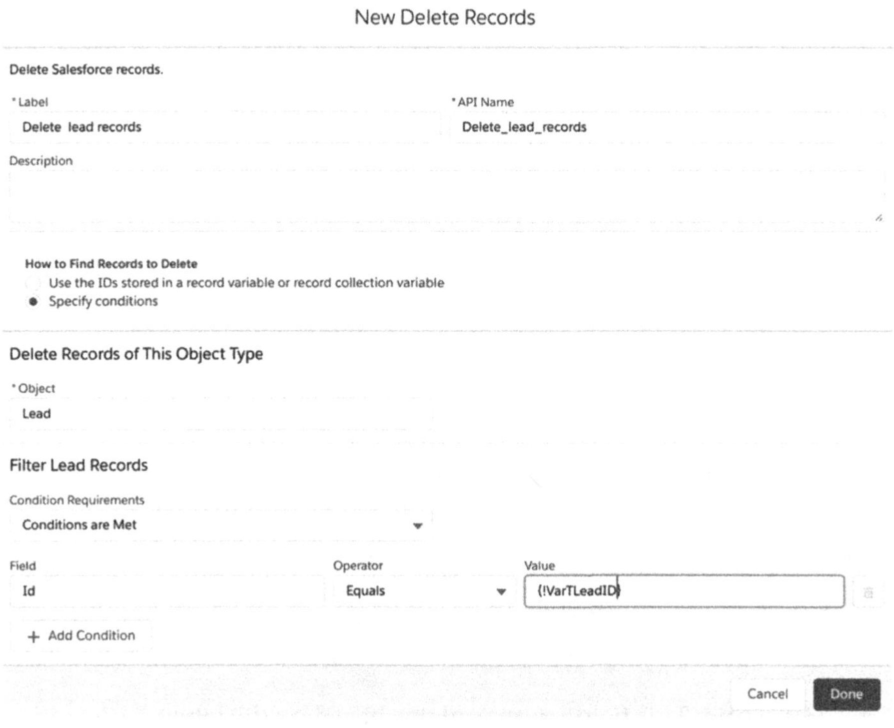

New Delete Records

Delete Salesforce records.

* Label	* API Name
Delete lead records	Delete_lead_records

Description

How to Find Records to Delete
  Use the IDs stored in a record variable or record collection variable
  ● Specify conditions

Delete Records of This Object Type

* Object
Lead

Filter Lead Records

Condition Requirements
Conditions are Met

Field	Operator	Value
Id	Equals	{!VarTLeadID}

+ Add Condition

Cancel   Done

Figure 6-14. *Configuring a* `Delete Records` *element*

8. When she is finished, Pamela clicks the `Done` button.

9. Now she needs to connect the `Delete Records` element with the `Start` element so that, at runtime, Lightning Flow can decide the order of execution of the elements. To do this, in the source element, Pamela finds the node at the bottom and then drags it to the target element (Figure 6-15).

Start

Delete Records
Delete lead records

Figure 6-15. *Connecting the flow elements*

10. Pamela clicks the Save button and enters Delete unqualified
    leads as the name by which to save the flow.

11. Pamela does not forget to activate the flow! She does so by clicking
    the Activate button.

Tip   To learn more about Lightning Flow, refer to this Trailhead module:
https://trailhead.salesforce.com/en/content/learn/modules/
business_process_automation.

Introduction to Lightning Process Builder

Lightning Process Builder is another way to automate business processes. It is the
upgraded version of workflow rules, which don't have capabilities to post a message on
chatter, create a child record on a specific action, autosubmit records for approval, and
so on. Process Builder supports these actions.

Lightning Process Builder is much more powerful than a workflow rule. It has the
capability to create a record or update the parent record if a lookup relationship exists
between the two objects. For example, if you want to automate a process of submitting
records into an approval process, without any manual intervention, you can use Process
Builder to do so.

Actions Process Builder Supports

Process Builder not only performs almost all activities available in workflow rules, but
it also consists of a few new actions. Unfortunately Process Builder doesn't support
outbound messages. You can use Process Builder to perform the following actions:

- **Apex**: Use this action to call the Apex class that contains the @ InvocableMethod annotation.

- **Create a Record**: Use this action to create a record. For example, create a lead when an opportunity is updated as Closed Lost.

- **E-mail Alerts**: Use this action to send out e-mail alerts to notify users or customers.

- **Flows**: Use this action to call a flow.

- **Post to Chatter**: Use this action to post a message on a chatter group, record feed, or on a user's chatter feed.

- **Processes**: Use this action to invoke a process from another process.

- **Quick Actions**: Use this action to create a record, update a record, or log a call by using a quick action—either object specific or global.

- **Quip**: Use this action to automate Quip documentation. For example, autocreate a Quip document when a new account is created.

- **Send Custom Notification**: Use this action to send a custom notification to your users on the Salesforce mobile app or inside Lightning Experience.

- **Send Survey Invitation**: Use this action to autosend a survey invitation to customers.

- **Submit for Approval**: Use this action to autosubmit a record to an approval process.

- **Update Records**: Use this action to update one or more records related to the record that started the process.

When to Use Which Automation Tool

Salesforce provides numerous tools to automate business processes, such as Lightning Flow, workflow rules, and Process Builder. It is vital to understand the differences among these tools and know when to use which tool. Table 6-1 presents the differences among these tools.

Table 6-1. *Differences among Automation Tools*

	Workflow Rule	Lightning Flow	Lightning Process Builder
Visual Designer	Not available	Available	Available
Starts when	Record is created or edited	• Manually • Automatically through Process Builder • At a specified time	Record is created or edited
Supports time-based actions	Yes	Yes	Yes
Calls Apex code	No	Yes	Yes
Creates records	Only task	Yes	Yes
Updates records	Yes (only fields from the same record or parent, in the case of a master detail relationship)	Yes, any record	Yes, any related record
Deletes records	No	Yes	No
Launches a flow	No	Yes	Yes
Posts to chatter	No	Yes	Yes, only text posts
Sends an e-mail	Yes	Yes	Yes
Submits for approval	No	Yes	Yes
Sends outbound messages	Yes	No	No
Supports user interaction	No	Yes	No
Supports version control	No	Yes	Yes
Supports user input at runtime	No	Yes (using the `Screen` element)	No

Use Case 3: Call an Autolaunched Flow

Pamela Kline created an autolaunched flow in use case 2. Now she wants to learn how it can be invoked from Process Builder when a lead is marked as unqualified. She performs the following steps to call a flow using Lightning Process Builder:

1. She navigates to Setup (gear icon) ➤ Setup ➤ Process Automation ➤ Process Builder to create a new process from scratch. Then she clicks the New Button available on the Process Management page. A pop-up appears where she enters the following details:

    a. **Name**: She enters the name for the process (Delete unqualified leads pb). Pamela knows the name must be no more than 255 characters.

    b. **API Name**: This field autopopulates based on the name.

    c. **Description**: Pamela writes some meaningful text so other developers and administrators can understand easily why this process was created.

    d. **The process starts when**: She selects A record changes.

2. When done, she clicks the Save button.

3. Next Pamela needs to select the object on which she wants to create a process. To do so, she clicks the Object node, which opens a window where she enters the following details:

    a. **Object**: Pamela starts typing and then selects the Lead object.

    b. **Start the process**: She selects when a record is created or edited.

    c. **Allow process to evaluate a record multiple times in a single transaction**: Pamela knows that you select this check box only if you want the process to evaluate the same record up to five times in a single transaction. It might reexamine the record because a process, workflow rule, or flow updated the record in the same transaction. Finally, her process looks like Figure 6-16.

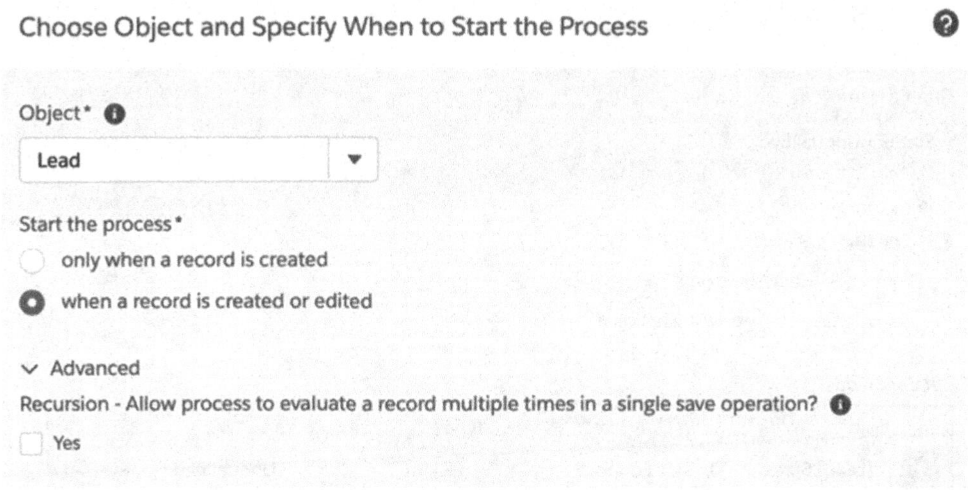

Choose Object and Specify When to Start the Process   ❓

Object* ⓘ

Lead   ▼

Start the process*

○ only when a record is created

◉ when a record is created or edited

⌄ Advanced

Recursion - Allow process to evaluate a record multiple times in a single save operation? ⓘ

☐ Yes

Figure 6-16. *Configuring evaluation criteria*

4. When done, she clicks the Save button.

5. The next task is to add process criteria so the process always fires
    when the lead status is unqualified. To define the process criteria,
    Pamela clicks the +Add Criteria node, which opens a window
    where she enters the following details:

    a. **Criteria Name**: Pamela enters a name for the criteria node.
        Here, she enters Status = Unqualified as the criteria name.

    b. **Criteria for Executing Actions**: Here, she can select the type of
        criteria she wants to define. Pamela can use a formula or filter
        to define the process criteria, or she could opt for no criteria. In
        this case, Pamela selects Conditions are met, which means
        the process will fire when the lead status is unqualified.

    c. **Do you want to execute the actions only when specified
        changes are made to the record?** Pamela selects this option
        because she wants the execution to happen only once, when
        the condition is met for the first time, not every time a record is
        edited.

Finally, her process looks like Figure 6-17.

Define Criteria for this Action Group

Criteria Name* ⓘ

Status = Unqualified

Criteria for Executing Actions*

◉ Conditions are met

◯ Formula evaluates to true

◯ No criteria–just execute the actions!

Set Conditions

	Field*		Operator*		Type*		Value*	
1	[Lead].Status	Q	Equals	▼	Picklist	▼	Unqualified	▼ ✕

+ Add Row

Conditions*

◉ All of the conditions are met (AND)

◯ Any of the conditions are met (OR)

◯ Customize the logic

∨ Advanced

Do you want to execute the actions only when specified changes are made to the record? ⓘ

☑ Yes

Save   Cancel

Figure 6-17. *Configuring process criteria*

6. When done, she clicks the Save button.

7. Next, Pamela must add one immediate action to call an autolaunched flow. To do this, she selects the Flows action available in the Action Type field. She clicks Add Action, which is available under IMMEDIATE ACTIONS, and configures it as shown in Figure 6-18.

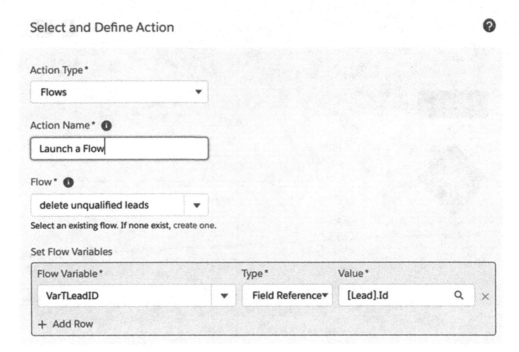

Figure 6-18. *Configuring the* Flows *action*

> To select the fields, she could use Field Picker; to enter the
> value, she could use the Text Entry field.

8. When done, Pamela clicks the Save button. In the end, her process
    looks like Figure 6-19.

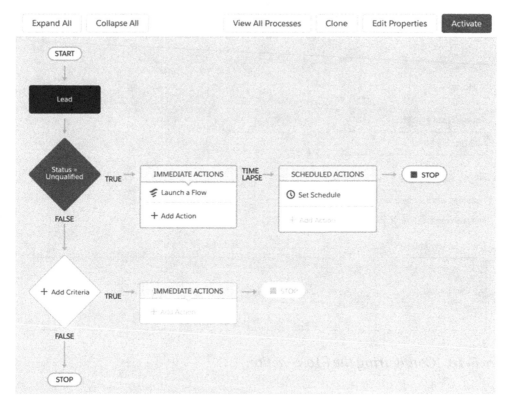

Figure 6-19. *Final version of the process*

9. Pamela does not forget to activate the process! She does so by clicking the `Activate` button.

The next time a user updates a lead to unqualified, the process Pamela created (using Process Builder) will fire and delete the record.

Use Case 4: Update Child Records

Pamela receives another requirement from her manager: when an opportunity is updated as `Closed Lost`, update all related quotes to `Denied`.

There are several ways to meet this requirement:

- Use an Apex trigger

- Use a combination of Lightning Flow and Lightning Process Builder

- Use a combination of Lightning Flow and Inline Visualforce Page on the Opportunity detail page

- Use Lightning Process Builder

Pamela decides to use Process Builder because it is fast and doesn't require coding skills. She performs the following steps:

1. She navigates to Setup (gear icon) ➤ Setup ➤ Process Automation ➤ Process Builder to create a new process from scratch. She clicks the New button available on the Process Management page. A pop-up appears and she enters the following details:

   a. **Name**: She enters the process name Update quotes. She knows the name must be no more than 255 characters.

   b. **API Name**: This field autopopulates based on the name.

   c. **Description**: Pamela writes some meaningful text so other developers and administrators can understand easily why this process was created.

   d. **The process starts when**: She selects A record changes.

2. When done, she clicks the Save button.

3. Now Pamela needs to select the object on which she wants to create a process. She clicks the Object node, which opens a window where she enters the following details:

   a. **Object**: She starts typing and then selects the Opportunity object.

   b. **Start the process**: She selects when a record is created or edited.

   c. **Allow process to evaluate a record multiple times in a single transaction**: Pamela knows that you select this check box only if you want the process to evaluate the same record up to five times in a single transaction. It might reexamine the record because a process, workflow rule, or flow updated the record in the same transaction.

4. When done, she clicks the Save button.

5. The next task is to add process criteria so the process always fires when the lead status is unqualified. To define the process criteria, Pamela clicks the +Add Criteria node, which opens a window where she enters the following details:

   a. **Criteria Name**: She enters Stage = Closed Lost as the criteria name.

   b. **Criteria for Executing Actions**: Here, Pamela can select the type of criteria she wants to define. She can either use a formula or filter to define the process criteria, or she can choose no criteria. In this case, she selects Conditions are met and opts for Stage = Closed Lost, which means the process fires when the opportunity stage is Closed Lost.

   c. **Do you want to execute the actions only when specified changes are made to the record?** Pamela selects this option because she wants the execution to happen only once, when the condition is met for the first time, not every time a record is edited.

Finally, her screen looks like Figure 6-20.

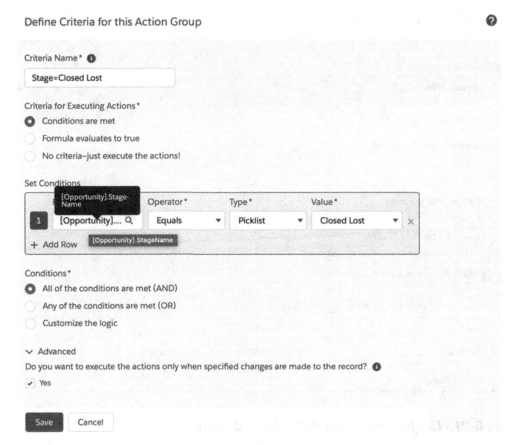

Figure 6-20. *Configuring process criteria*

6.   When done, she clicks the Save button.

7.   Next, Pamela must add one immediate action to call an autolaunched flow. To do this, Pamela uses the Update Records action available in the Action Type field. She clicks Add Action, which is available under IMMEDIATE ACTIONS, and configures it as shown in Figure 6-21.

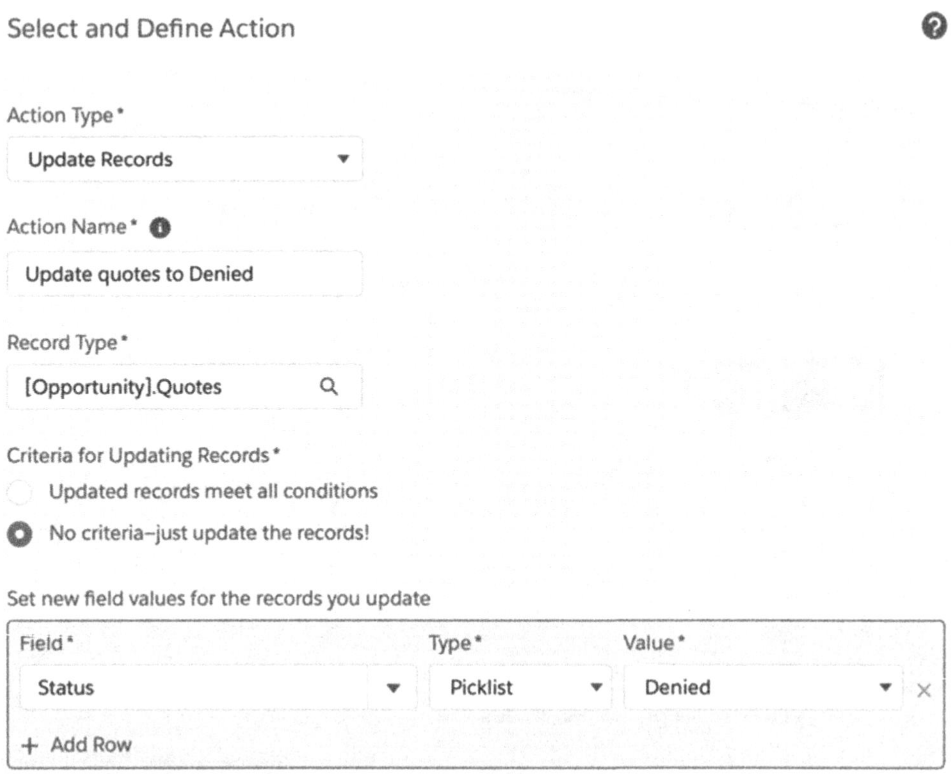

Select and Define Action   ❓

Action Type *

    Update Records   ▼

Action Name * ⓘ

    Update quotes to Denied

Record Type *

    [Opportunity].Quotes   🔍

Criteria for Updating Records *

    ⚪ Updated records meet all conditions

    🔘 No criteria–just update the records!

Set new field values for the records you update

Field *		Type *		Value *		
Status	▼	Picklist	▼	Denied	▼	✕
+ Add Row						

Figure 6-21. *Configuring the Update Records action*

> To select the fields, Pamela can use Field Picker; to enter the
> value, she can use the Text Entry field.

8. When done, she clicks the Save button. In the end, her process
    looks like Figure 6-22.

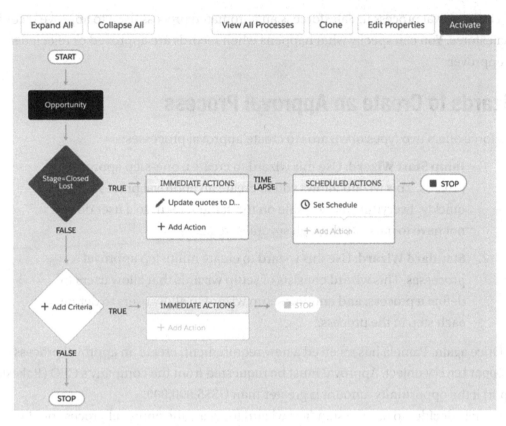

Figure 6-22. *Final version of the process*

9. Pamela does not forget to activate the process! She does so by
   clicking the Activate button.

The next time a user updates an opportunity to Closed Lost, the process Pamela
created (using Process Builder) fires and set quotes to Denied.

Introduction to Approval Processes

Almost every organization uses some sort of approval process. For example, if you want
to take a day or two off, you may need to get approval from your manager to do so. An
approval process is a way an organization approves anything from invoices, budgets, and
purchase orders to a new process the company wants to incorporate. Implementing an
approval process can standardize an organization's internal processes, and also saves
time by creating a dependable, repeatable process. Approval processes are a type of
workflow, which is any sequence of work from initiation to completion, that you can
create to ensure work is approved the same way every time.

The approval process in Salesforce is an automated process used to approve records in Salesforce. You can specify what happens when records are approved or rejected by the approver.

Wizards to Create an Approval Process

Salesforce offers two types of wizards to create approval processes:

1. **Jump Start Wizard**: Use this wizard to create a one-step approval process. This wizard allows you to create an approval process quickly. Everything is available on the same screen, so a user does not have to navigate through several screens.

2. **Standard Wizard**: Use this wizard to create multistep approval processes. This wizard consists of setup wizards that allow users to define a process, and another setup wizard to allow users to define each step in the process.

Once again, Pamela has received a new requirement: create an approval process on the Opportunity object. Approval must be requested from the company's CEO (Rakesh Gupta) if the opportunity amount is greater than US$5,000,000.

Pamela decides to use the standard wizard to create the approval process on the Opportunity object. Before proceeding, she makes sure she has the Approval Status picklist on the Opportunity object, as shown in Table 6-2.

Table 6-2. *Create a Custom Field*

Field Type	Label	Length/Values
Picklist	Status	Submitted
		Approved
		Rejected

Creating a New Approval Process

Pamela performs the following steps in Lightning Experience to create a new approval process on the Opportunity object:

1. She navigates to Setup (gear icon) ➤ All Setup ➤ PLATFORM TOOLS ➤ Process Automation ➤ Approval Processes.

2. From the Manage Approval Processes For drop-down, she selects the Opportunity object.

3. Next, she selects Create new approval process from the drop-down, then selects Use Standard Setup Wizard.

4. Then she enters the following information:

   a. **Process Name**: Pamela types $5M deal approval process.

   b. **Unique Name**: This field is autopopulated based on the process name.

   c. **Description**: Pamela enter a meaningful description of the approval process so other administrators can understand easily why this approval process was created.

5. When done, she clicks the Next button.

6. Now Pamela must specify the entry criteria. When done, her screen looks like Figure 6-23.

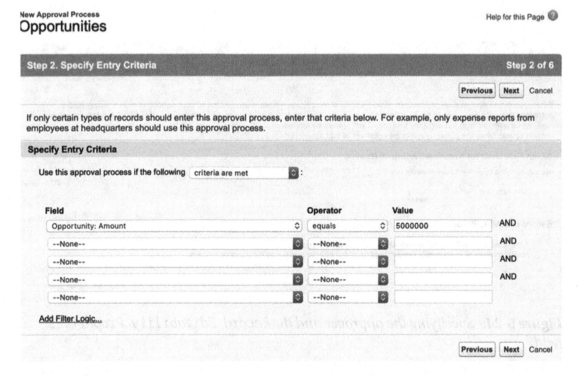

Figure 6-23. *Specifying entry criteria*

When done, she clicks the Next button.

7. Now Pamela must define the following actions:

a. **Select Field Used for Automated Approval Routing**: The approval process allows an approval process creator to assign approval requests to any user. Another option is to use a user field to route approval requests automatically. The user field can be any custom hierarchical relationship field, such as Reporting Manager or the manager standard user field. Pamela leaves this as is.

b. **Record Editability Properties**: When a record is submitted for approval, it gets locked. The process allows Pamela to define who can edit the record when a record is in the midst of an approval process. She selects the option Administrators OR the currently assigned approver can edit records during the approval process.

Pamela's screen looks like Figure 6-24.

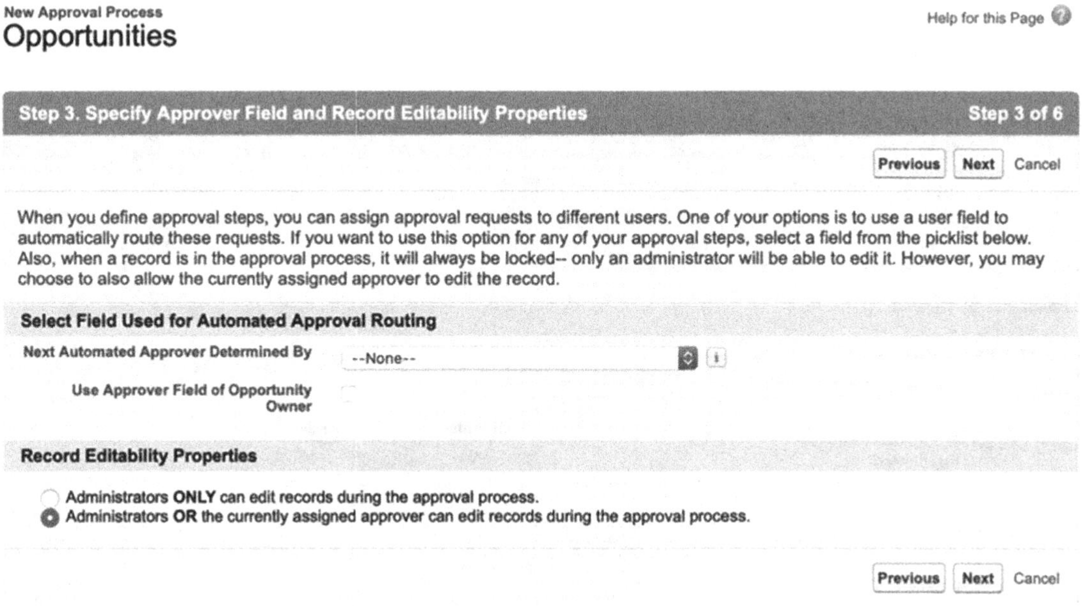

New Approval Process
Opportunities

Help for this Page

Step 3. Specify Approver Field and Record Editability Properties   Step 3 of 6

Previous Next Cancel

When you define approval steps, you can assign approval requests to different users. One of your options is to use a user field to automatically route these requests. If you want to use this option for any of your approval steps, select a field from the picklist below. Also, when a record is in the approval process, it will always be locked-- only an administrator will be able to edit it. However, you may choose to also allow the currently assigned approver to edit the record.

Select Field Used for Automated Approval Routing

Next Automated Approver Determined By   --None--

Use Approver Field of Opportunity Owner

Record Editability Properties

◯ Administrators **ONLY** can edit records during the approval process.
⦿ Administrators **OR** the currently assigned approver can edit records during the approval process.

Previous Next Cancel

Figure 6-24. *Specifying the approver and the* Record Editability Properties *field*

When done, she clicks the Next button.

8. When an approval process assigns an approval request to a user, it automatically sends an e-mail notification to the user. The e-mail contains a link to the approval page. If you want to use your custom e-mail template, then choose a template or leave it blank. If you leave it blank, Salesforce uses the default e-mail template. When done, Pamela clicks the Next button.

9. On the next screen, Select Fields to Display on Approval Page Layout, Pamela does the following:

   a. She selects the fields she wants to display on the Approval Request page.

   b. She selects the check box Display approval history information in addition to the fields selected above to display the approval history-related list on the Approval Request page.

   c. In the Security Settings section, Pamela must select the option where users can approve or reject a request. She selects Allow approvers to access the approval page from within the salesforce.com application, or externally from a wireless-enabled mobile device.

Her screen looks like Figure 6-25.

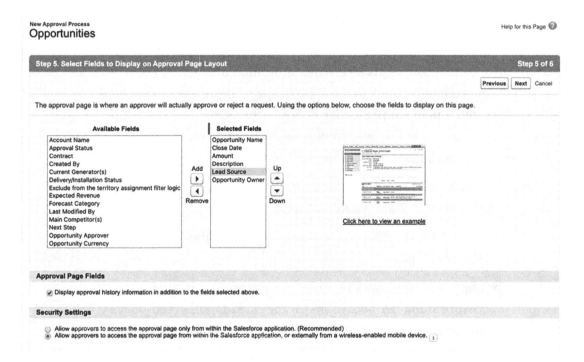

Figure 6-25. *Selecting fields to display on the Approval Request page*

When done, Pamela clicks the Next button.

10. Now Pamela must specify the initial submitters (Figure 6-26). She does this as follows:

   a. In the Submitter Type section, she selects Opportunity Owner.

   b. Then she selects the check box Add the Approval History related list to all Registration page layouts to add the approval history-related list to the Account page.

   c. Pamela then makes sure she selects the check box Allow submitters to recall approval requests. This will allow the submitter to recall the approval process.

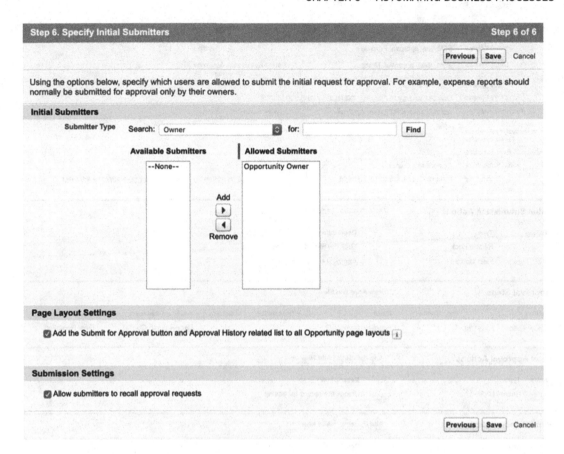

Figure 6-26. *Specifying initial submitters*

11. When done, she clicks the Save button. In the next screen, she
     selects the option No, I'll do this later, take me back to
     the listing of all approval processes for this object.
     The system redirects her to the screen shown in Figure 6-27.

Process Definition Detail   Edit ▾ | Clone | Delete | Activate

Process Name	$5M deal approval Process		Active
Unique Name	X5M_deal_approval_Process	Next Automated Approver Determined By	
Description			
Entry Criteria	Opportunity: Amount EQUALS "USD 5,000,000"		
Record Editability	Administrator **OR** Current Approver	Allow Submitters to Recall Approval Requests	✓
Approval Assignment Email Template			
Approval Post Template			
Initial Submitters	Opportunity Owner		
Created By	Rakesh Gupta, 9/8/2019 1:37 PM	Modified By	Rakesh Gupta, 10/3/2019 4:51 PM

Initial Submission Actions ⓘ   Add Existing | Add New ▾

Action	Type	Description
	Record Lock	Lock the record from being edited
Edit	Remove	Field Update	Approval status = Submitted

Approval Steps ⓘ   New Approval Step

Action	Step Number	Name	Description	Criteria	Assigned Approver	Reject Behavior
Show Actions	Edit	Del	1	Approval from CEO			User:Rakesh Gupta	Final Rejection

Final Approval Actions ⓘ   Add Existing | Add New ▾

Action	Type	Description
Edit	Record Lock	Unlock the record for editing

Final Rejection Actions ⓘ   Add Existing | Add New ▾

Action	Type	Description
Edit	Record Lock	Unlock the record for editing

Recall Actions ⓘ   Add Existing | Add New ▾

Action	Type	Description
	Record Lock	Unlock the record for editing

Figure 6-27. *Approval process detail page*

Final Approval Actions

Final approval happens only when a record has received all the required approvals. For the current scenario, Pamela navigates to the Final Approval Actions section, then clicks the Edit link and selects Unlock the record for editing, as shown in Figure 6-28.

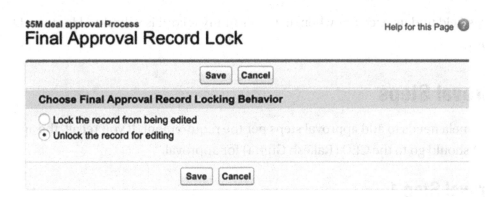

Figure 6-28. Final approval action

When done, she clicks the Save button. She repeats these steps for the Final Rejection and Recall actions.

Initial Submission Actions

The Initial action happens only when a record is initially submitted for approval. When the record is submitted successfully for approval, it gets locked. You can define actions such as Field Update, Email Alert, Assign Task, and Outbound Message. Add one initial submission action to update the Approval Status field to Submitted, as shown in Figure 6-29.

Field Update Edit	Save	Save & New	Cancel	
Identification				❚ = Required Information

Name	Approval status = Submitte
Unique Name	Approval_status_Submittec ⓘ
Namespace Prefix	rakeshistomMVP
Description	
Object	Opportunity
Protected Component	☐
Field to Update	Approval Status ◇
Field Data Type	Picklist
Re-evaluate Workflow Rules after Field Change	☐ⓘ

Specify New Field Value

Picklist Options
- ☐ The value above the current one
- ☐ The value below the current one
- ◉ A specific value Submitted ◇

Figure 6-29. Initial submission action

This field update executes when an Opportunity record is submitted for the CEO's approval.

Approval Steps

Now Pamela needs to add approval steps per the requirement. If you recall, the approval request should go to the CEO (Rakesh Gupta) for approval.

Approval Step 1

The first step is to get the approval from the CEO (Rakesh Gupta). Pamela performs the following actions to achieve this:

1. She navigates to the Approval Steps section then clicks the New Approval Step button.

2. Next, she enters the following details:

   a. **Name**: Pamela types Approval from CEO.

   b. **Unique Name**: The unique name is autopopulated based on the name.

   c. **Description**: Pamela enters a meaningful description of the approval step so other developers and administrators can understand easily why this second approval step has been created.

   d. When done, she clicks the Next button.

3. Now Pamela needs to filter out records. She decides which record should enter the approval step. She can filter out a record by adding more conditions. For example, suppose she wants to filter the Opportunity record that is refereed by partners. For this scenario, she would select All records should enter this step, then click the Next button.

4. In the next screen, Pamela selects User ➤ Rakesh Gupta. Her screen now looks like Figure 6-30.

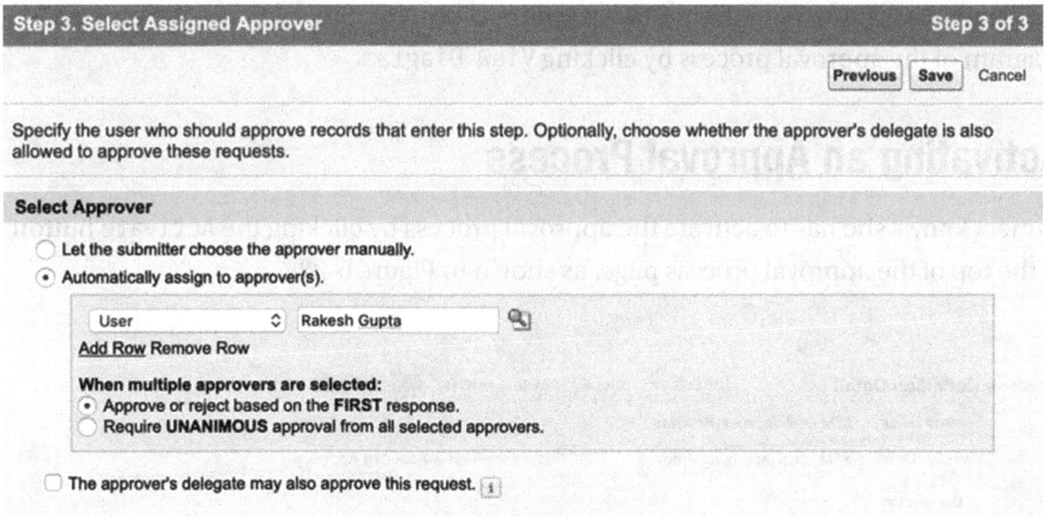

Figure 6-30. *Selecting an assigned approver*

5.   When done, she clicks the Save button.

6.   On the next screen she selects the option No, I'll do this later. Take me to the approval process detail page to review what I've just created. Pamela is then redirected to the approval process detail page.

7.   Now she adds field updates to the Approval Actions and Rejection Actions sections to update the Status field to Approved or Rejected, as shown in Figure 6-31.

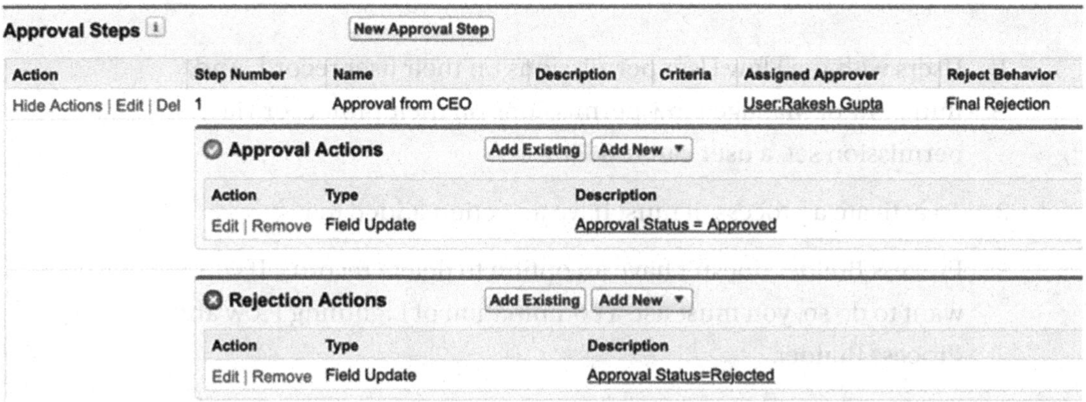

Figure 6-31. *Field updates to show* Approval *or* Rejection *actions*

Pamela has now created a multistep approval process. She can view the process diagram of the approval process by clicking `View Diagram`.

Activating an Approval Process

Pamela knows she has to activate the approval process by clicking the `Activate` button at the top of the approval process page, as shown in Figure 6-32.

Figure 6-32. *Activating an approval process*

Before activating it, however, she makes sure no more changes are required, because once an approval process is active, it is not possible to add more steps to it.

Points to Remember

1. Users with the Flow User permissions on their user record. And, Run Flow or Manage Flow permissions on their profile, or via a permission set, a user can run Flow.

2. To activate a process, it must have an action added to it.

3. Process Builder doesn't have an option to delete records. If you want to do so, you must use a combination of Lightning Flow and Process Builder.

4. The process/flow owner, or last modified user, receives an e-mail from Salesforce if the process fails during runtime or if any other fault occurs. Use the Apex `Exception Email` option to distribute such errors to other users.

5. A process has same the governing limits as that of Apex.

6. Process actions are executed in the same order in which they appear in the process.

7. You can't delete an active process. If you want to do so, you must first deactivate it.

8. If you leave the `Next Automated Approver Determined By` field blank, you can't assign approval requests automatically to the manager in any step you create for an approval process.

9. You can use Process Builder to autosubmit the record into an approval process.

10. Use the Mass Transfer Approval Requests wizard to "mass-transfer" pending approval requests from one user to another user.

11. You can create and run approval history reports to check in-progress and completed approval processes and their steps.

Hands-on Exercises

The following exercises will give you more practice with the platform, which ultimately will help you in gaining mastery of it, and also will assist you in preparing for the certification examination. Remember, these are hands-on exercises, and you can find the answers at the back of the book in the Appendix, but try to implement them in your Salesforce org, which is the primary goal of doing them. Try to do the exercises without looking at the answers!

1. Create a flow that displays three number fields: `First Number`, `Second Number`, and `Third Number`. On the next screen, show the summation of the values in these fields.

2.   Dennis Williams, a system administrator at GoC, receives a requirement to send a welcome e-mail to new customers (contacts) as soon as a user is created in Salesforce. How would you instruct him to meet this requirement?

3.   Dennis Williams receives another requirement to keep the contact's phone number in sync with the account's `Phone Number` field. This means, whenever someone updates a phone number on an account, it should be reflected in the contact's record. How would you instruct him to meet this requirement?

4.   Dennis wants to implement opportunity management at GoC, but he is a bit confused by one of the requirements. Because you now have a better understanding of process automation, please help him automate the business process for the following requirements:

   a.   When an opportunity amount is greater than $1,000,000, create a post on the chatter group Key Deals.

   b.   Whenever an opportunity is marked `Closed Won`, autoupdate the account description to `We won another deal!`

   c.   Whenever an opportunity is marked `Closed Won`, notify the opportunity team on Salesforce mobile and in Lightning Experience.

5.   Dennis Williams receives a requirement to add the permission set `View All Leads` automatically to new users. How would you instruct him to meet this requirement?

Summary

In this chapter, we covered Lightning Flow, and Lightning Flow Designer and its life cycle. We also went through different use cases of Lightning Flow. Furthermore, we reviewed Lightning Process Builder via a few examples. Last, we studied approval processes and how to configure them by looking at an example. In Chapter 7, we examine the application development life cycle. So, stay tuned!

CHAPTER 7

Nuts and Bolts of Application Development

In Chapter 6, we covered Lightning Flow, followed by an in-depth overview of Lightning Process Builder. We also examined approval processes using real-life examples.

This chapter consists of three parts. In part one, we look at limits of declarative customization and when to use programmatic development. In part two, we examine the application development life cycle, including different types of sandboxes and deployment tools. In part three, we study different deployment tools.

Limits of Declarative Development

As awesome as out-of-the-box point-and-click features are, there are limits to their reach. For example, we've studied formula fields, validation rules, Process Builder, page layouts, and so on. These point-and-click tools make Salesforce even better, allowing for easy configuration and maintenance. The problem arises when one gets requirements that cannot be solved using out-of-the box features.

Business Use Case 1

Pamela Kline is still working as a salesforce administrator at GoC. She has discovered that sales reps are deleting Closed Lost opportunities, which is detrimental to accurate analytics, to say the least! Pamela wants to make sure that sales reps are only allowed to delete those opportunities that are not Closed Won or Closed Lost.

© Rakesh Gupta 2020
R. Gupta, *Salesforce Platform App Builder Certification*, https://doi.org/10.1007/978-1-4842-5479-0_7

How should Pamela meet this business requirement? If your answer is to use a validation rule, take a few minutes to ask yourself: when would the validation rule fire?

A validation rule fires only when a record is created or edited, not when a record is deleted. So now you know that using a validation rule is not the right thing to do. This use case also reveals limitations of declarative solutions and indicates that we need to go beyond point-and-clicks toward code.

Solution: Use an Apex Trigger

There are several ways to meet Pamela's new business requirement, but the best way to do so is to write an Apex trigger on the Opportunity object, as follows:

```
trigger opportunityValidation(before delete){
    for(Opportunity opp: Trigger.new){
        if(opp.StageName == 'Closed Won' || opp.StageName == 'Closed Lost'){
            Opp.AddError(You are not allowed to delete closed won or closed
            lost opportunity);
        }
    }
}
```

A trigger is executed during Data Manipulation Language (DML) database actions. For example, you can create a trigger on the Account object that executes whenever an Account record is updated or deleted. Therefore, triggers are called implicitly from a database action.

Business Use Case 2

Pamela Kline just received another requirement from her manager: whenever a new account is approved in Salesforce, create a pdf and send it to all contacts on that account.

Let's take a few minutes to pause and think. Can we use a point-and-click solution here? If your answer is no, then you are on the right track!

Solution 1: Use a Visualforce Page

There are various solutions available in the market to generate pdf documents from Salesforce, but one thing they all have in common is that they are built using custom development.

To meet the requirement, Pamela (or her developer) can create a simple Visualforce page, as follows:

```
<apex:page showHeader="false" standardController="Account"
standardStylesheets="false" renderAs="PDF">
//Your logic goes here
</apex:page>
```

Visualforce is a framework that includes a tag-based markup language. It allows you to build sophisticated, attractive, and dynamic custom user interfaces. You can use almost all standard web technologies—such as, CSS, jQuery, and HTML5—with a Visualforce page. This means you can build a rich user interface for any device, including mobile, tablet, and so on.

Solution 2: Use an AppExchange App

An alternative solution for Pamela to meet the requirement is to use Salesforce AppExchange apps such as Conga, Drawloop, Nintex, DocGen, and so on.

Are you wondering whether it is better to write Apex code or use apps from an AppExchange app? The answer should always depend on availability of time, budget, and ability to meet expectations.

The pros and cons of using Apex vs. leveraging AppExchange are as follows: custom development offers flexibility and a highly tailored solution to meet your specific needs and expectations in a highly granular manner. However, precisely because of this, it may take longer to build and, as a result, may cost more. AppExchange apps, on the other hand, may not meet all of your needs completely, but the apps will be up and running in hours, if not minutes. And, as a result, the end product may be cheaper. In such a situation, the best practice is to do a gap analysis and, based on the outcome, opt for one or the other solution.

Business Use Case 3

Pamela's manager wants to provide detailed information about GoC's potential customers, such as the weather in the city where a contact resides, to sales reps. To achieve this, GoC wants to display weather information based on a contact's mailing city. What do you think? How should Pamela meet this requirement? Does Salesforce have any out-of-the box functionality to achieve this?

Solution: Use APIs

The answer to the previous question is, again, no. Unfortunately, Salesforce doesn't have any out-of-the-box functionality to meet Pamela's new requirement. So, the next question is: how should she meet the requirement? The answer is to use APIs. Yes, you got it right. API stand for application program interface. Web sites like Weather.com and AccWeather offer APIs so that developers can consume it and get the necessary information. Using APIs, it is possible to get weather information based on a customer's mailing location.

Use Case Summary

As the three scenarios discussed in this section show, the best practice is to assess the pros and cons of declarative customization vs programmatic development. When you start working on real projects or with a Trailhead module (which I strongly suggest), you will master the art of deciding the best path forward—be it declarative, programmatic, or both!

Managing the Application Life Cycle

Application life cycle management entails end-to-end management of the software development process. The process includes governance, development, and operation. The software development life cycle (also known as SDLC), on the other hand, focuses primarily on the development phase.

Depending on your software development methodology (waterfall, Agile, or DevOps), application life cycle management might be split into separate phases or may be fully integrated into a continuous delivery process. Regardless, application life cycle management can be broken down into three category: governance, development, and operations.

Application Governance

Application governance teams start by gathering requirements from business stakeholders. Architects or solution designers create design documentation. The team then hands over the document to a development team for implementation.

Application Development

Next comes the development stage of application life cycle management. SDLC includes building, testing, releasing the build, releasing the test, and updating the application.

Application Operations

The third step in application life cycle management is operations. Operations includes deployment of the application and maintenance of the technology (which is not applicable in Salesforce).

Sandboxes

No sandbox comes with a developer org. Fortunately, we have used Salesforce's free developer edition org to perform the tasks and exercises in this book. Because developer orgs are yours forever, you can keep practicing in such orgs even if you switch jobs.

This, however, is not the same when you work on your company's org. You lose access to the org when you switch jobs. The advantage of being on a company's Salesforce org is that you get access to at least one sandbox org. A sandbox is like a developer org except that it is affiliated with a company's production org. A sandbox allows you to build and test business processes in a controlled environment without negatively impacting your production org. When you know your workflow rules, formula fields, and flows are working correctly in a sandbox, you can migrate them to your production org. You can create a sandbox from production or from a live org.

The question is: why do we need a sandbox when we have a free developer org? Here is my answer: a free developer org comes with a few limitations—for example:

1.   Data storage: 5MB

2.   File storage: 20MB

3.   Salesforce licenses: 2

4.   A fewer number of API calls per day

When you start working on a real project, you may need a playground that allows you to work with more data and file storage, including more API calls per day, and more Salesforce licenses so you can create more than two user accounts, if required.

There are different types of sandboxes and they are summarized in Table 7-1.

Table 7-1. *Sandbox Types and Their Differences*

Sandbox Type	Refresh Interval	Storage Limit	Sandbox Template	What Copied
Developer	1 day	Data storage: 200MB File storage: 200MB	No	Metadata only
Developer Pro	1 day	Data storage: 1GB File storage: 1GB	No	Metadata only
Partial copy	5 days	Data storage: 5GB File storage: 5GB	Required	Metadata and sample data
Full	29 days	Same as your production org	Available	Metadata and all data (or sample data, if a sandbox template is being used), and chatter and history (optional)

In Table 7-1, "metadata" means all configurations, Apex code, and all users. The refresh interval is often referred to when discussing sandboxes. To "refresh" a sandbox means to copy fresh information from other sandboxes or a production org.

Let's look at the different types of available sandboxes more closely to help you choose the sandbox you would use for a project.

Developer Sandbox

Use a developer sandbox for isolated development purposes. In general, each organization has a good volume of such sandboxes. If you have seven developers working on a project, you can create seven developer sandboxes and give a separate sandbox to each developer. This eliminates the possibility of developers overwriting each others' work. This sandbox includes your production org's metadata (Apex, all users, and other configurations). A developer sandbox can be refreshed once a day.

Developer Pro Sandbox

Like the developer sandbox, the dev pro sandbox is used for development, Apex testing, and unit testing. A dev pro sandbox has a higher storage limit compared to a developer sandbox. Higher limits allow developers to test an application with larger data sets. Like a developer sandbox, a dev pro sandbox also includes your production org's meta data (Apex, all users, and configurations). And it can be refreshed once a day too.

Partial Sandbox

A partial sandbox contains a subset of data from your production org. The specific subset of data you include in the partial sandbox is defined in a sandbox template. A partial sandbox can be used for user acceptance testing, regression testing, and so forth. Unlike a developer sandbox and a dev pro sandbox, a partial sandbox can only be refreshed every five days.

Full Sandbox

A full sandbox is a replica of your production org. It can contain metadata such as attachments, object records, as well as users. In addition, it can also include chatter and field history data. This type of sandbox is used for integration testing, staging, and production debugging. It can be refreshed every 29 days.

Setting up a Sandbox

Let's rejoin Pamela Kline, who has an understanding of the importance of sandboxes. She wants to set up a developer sandbox so she can do configuration there. Pamela performs the following steps to create a developer sandbox:

1. She navigates to Setup (gear icon) ➤ Setup ➤ Environments ➤ Sandboxes.

2. Next, Pamela clicks New Sandbox, as shown in Figure 7-1.

Figure 7-1. *Creating a new sandbox*

3. Pamela enters the sandbox name Dev1 and, from the Create From drop-down, she selects Production, as shown in Figure 7-2.

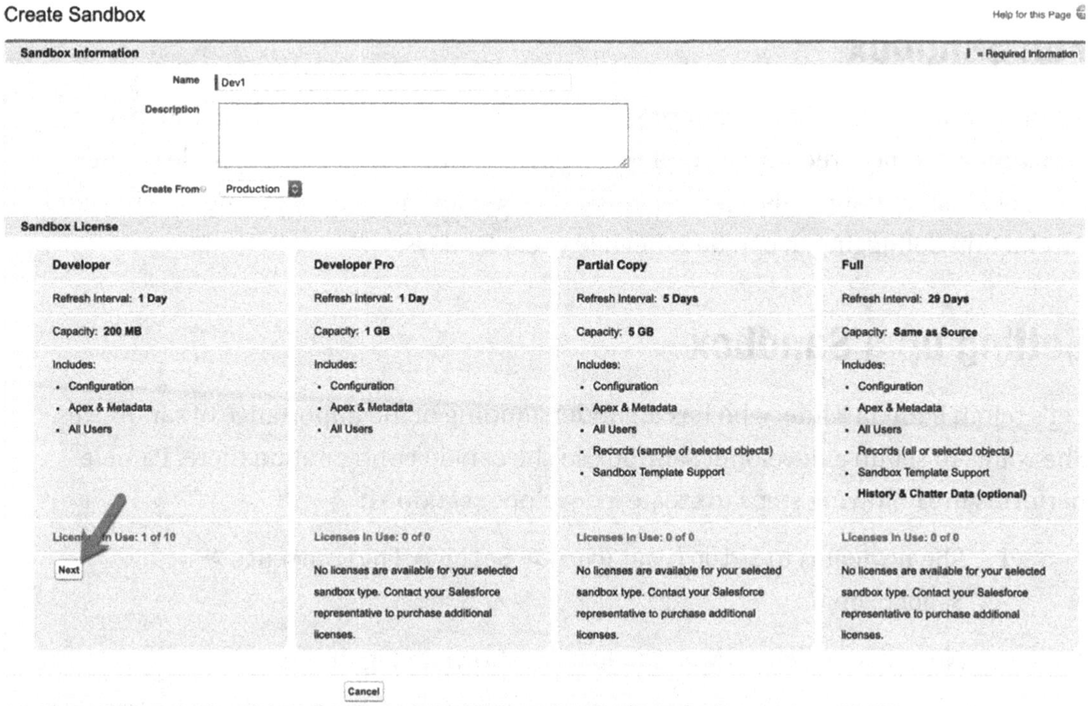

Figure 7-2. *Entering sandbox details*

4. Pamela clicks the Next button available in the Developer section. The system redirects Pamela to a new window to specify the Apex class she created previously from the SandboxPostCopy interface, which runs the scripts after each create and refresh for this sandbox. In this scenario, Pamela leaves this field blank, as shown in Figure 7-3.

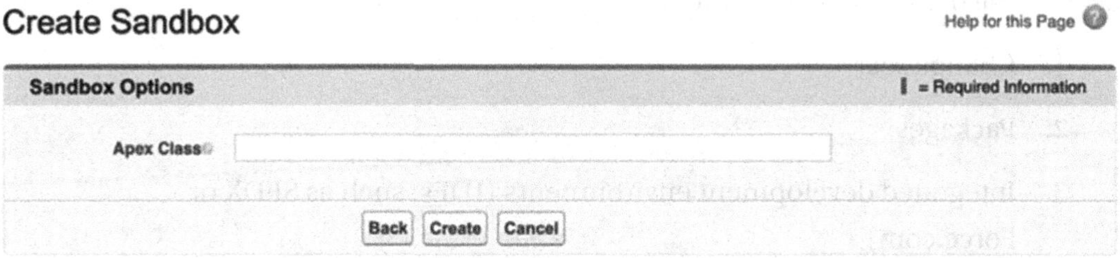

Create Sandbox

Help for this Page

Sandbox Options		▌ = Required Information
Apex Class		

Back Create Cancel

Figure 7-3. *Entering Apex class details*

5. When done, Pamela clicks the Create button, which starts the sandbox creation process. This process may take from several minutes to several days, depending on the size and type of your org.

Accessing a Sandbox

We've seen how to set up a sandbox, but how do we access one? If you recall, the setup process didn't ask us to set up a user account for our new sandbox!

Let's rejoin Pamela. She performs the following steps to access her newly created sandbox:

1. When the sandbox is ready, Pamela receives an e-mail from Salesforce to activate it, which she does.

2. The username is the production username appended by the sandbox name. For example, Pamela's production username is pamela@goc.com and the sandbox name is Dev1. As a result, the sandbox username is pamela@goc.com.dev1.

3. The password is the same as the production password.

Deployment

Pamela starts working in her newly created sandbox environment—the best way to configure or customize applications in Salesforce. She wants to understand how to move metadata to the production org from her sandbox.

When you create a field, or metadata, in a sandbox, it is not available automatically in the production org. To deploy the metadata between Salesforce environments, Pamela must use one of the following options:

1. Change sets

2. Packages

3. Integrated development environments (IDEs; such as SFDX or Force.com)

4. Force.com migration tool

5. Third-party deployment tools (such as Copado)

Deploy Using Change Sets

Change sets are the easiest way to deploy metadata between *connected* orgs. For example, you can use change sets to deploy a metadata component from sandbox to production, sandbox to sandbox, and production to sandbox.

Change sets include containers that hold metadata components. They can only be used to deploy *metadata components*, not data or records. To use change sets, make sure both organizations have a deployment connection setup. There are two types of change sets:

1. Outbound change sets

2. Inbound change sets

Outbound Change Sets

Outbound change sets can be used to send metadata components from a sandbox to production or to another sandbox.

Pamela, our hardworking system administrator, has created the custom field Anniversary Date on the Contact object in a sandbox. Now she wants to migrate the field to the production org. She performs the following steps to create an outbound change set:

1. She logs in to the sandbox environment by opening the URL `https://test.salesforce.com`.

2. She navigates to Setup (gear icon) ➤ Setup Home ➤ PLATFORM TOOLS ➤ Environments ➤ Change Sets ➤ Outbound Change Sets.

3. In the Change Sets section, she clicks the New button to create a new outbound change set, as shown in Figure 7-4.

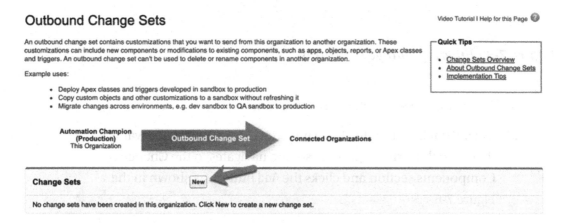

Figure 7-4. *Creating a new outbound change set*

4. This action opens a window, where she enters the following details:

   - **Name**: She enters a meaningful name for the outbound change set: Anniversary Date.

   - **Description**: Pamela writes some meaningful text so other developers and administrators can understand easily why this outbound change set was created in the first place.

   Her screen looks like Figure 7-5.

Change Set Edit
New Change Set

Change Set Edit   Save   Cancel

Name | Anniversary Date

Description

Save   Cancel

Figure 7-5. *Entering change set details*

5. When done, Pamela clicks the Save button.

6. Next, Pamela must add all the metadata components she wants to deploy to the target org. To do so, she navigates to the Change Set Components section and clicks the Add button, as shown in the Figure 7-6.

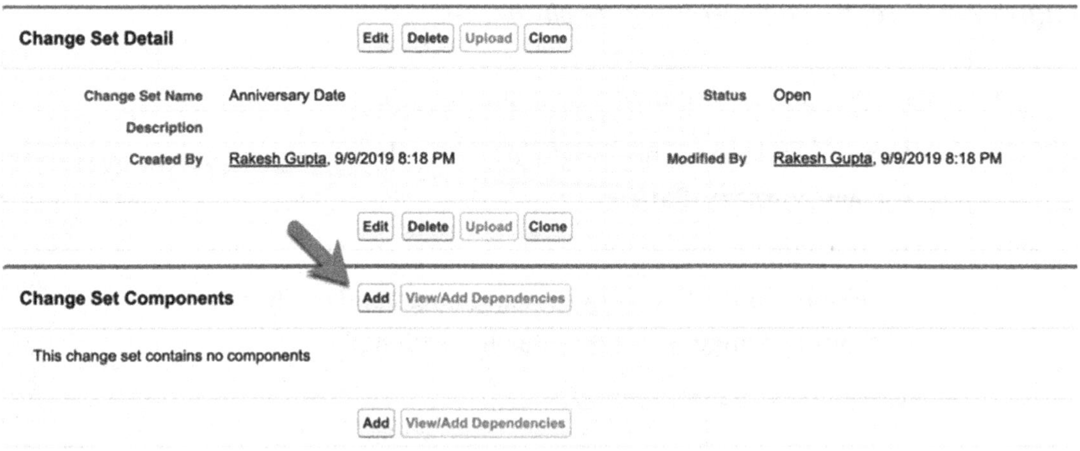

Change Set Detail   Edit   Delete   Upload   Clone

Change Set Name   Anniversary Date   Status   Open
Description
Created By   Rakesh Gupta, 9/9/2019 8:18 PM   Modified By   Rakesh Gupta, 9/9/2019 8:18 PM

Edit   Delete   Upload   Clone

Change Set Components   Add   View/Add Dependencies

This change set contains no components

Add   View/Add Dependencies

Figure 7-6. *Outbound change set components*

7. For Component Type, Pamela selects Custom Field. Then she
    selects the Anniversary Date field from the list, as shown in
    Figure 7-7.

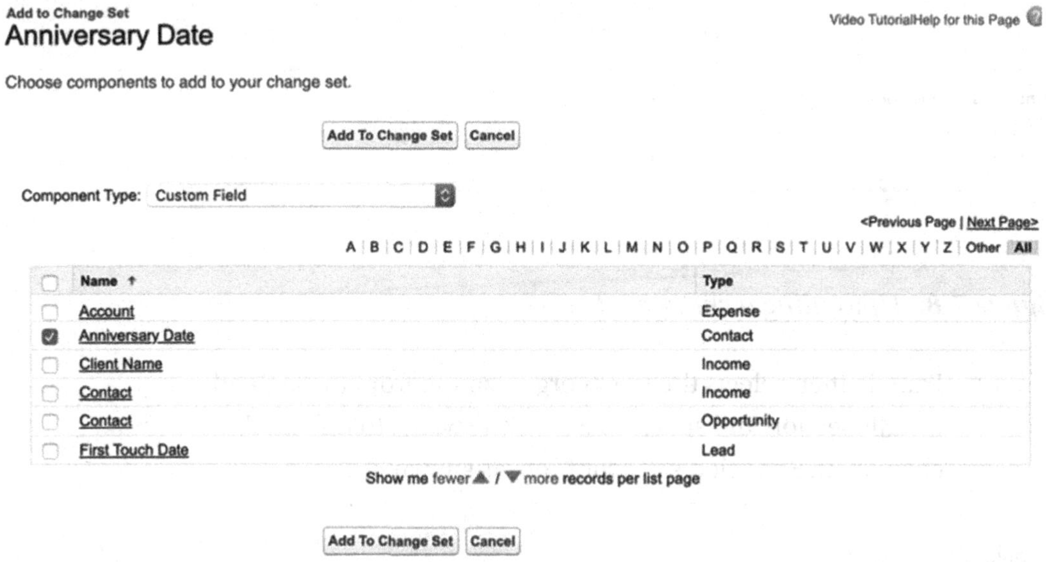

Figure 7-7. *Adding components to the change set*

8. When done, she clicks the Add To Change Set button. If Pamela
    had wanted to add multiple metadata components to her
    outbound change set, she would have repeated steps 6 and 7.

9. Pamela uploads the change set to the target (production) org. To
    do so, she navigates to the Change Set Detail section and then
    clicks Upload, as shown in Figure 7-8.

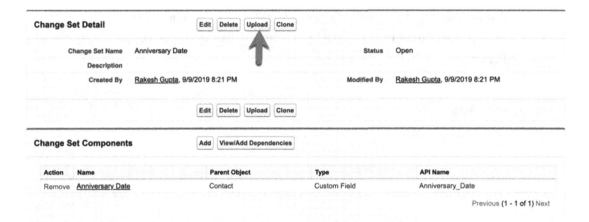

Figure 7-8. *Uploading a change set*

10. Pamela then selects the target organization from the Upload Details section and specifies where she wants to upload the change set. She selects `Production`, as shown in Figure 7-9.

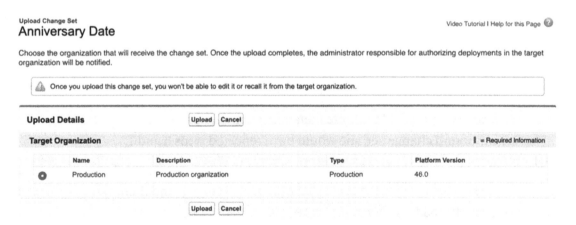

Figure 7-9. *Selecting a target org*

If, in the target org, inbound change set access was not granted for the current sandbox, Pamela wouldn't be able to select her target org from the list. In this case, she would have to return to the production and enable it.

11. When done, Pamela clicks the `Upload` button. If the upload is successful, she'll see a message onscreen, as shown in Figure 7-10. Pamela also receives and e-mail from Salesforce, affirming her change set upload was successful.

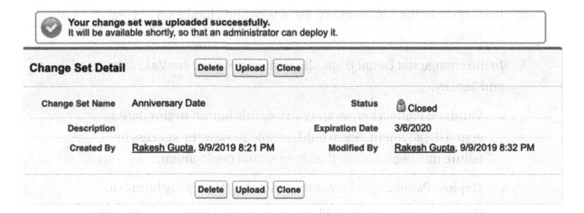

Figure 7-10. *Upload success message*

Inbound Change Sets

Inbound change sets can be used to receive metadata components from a sandbox to production or to other sandboxes. Pamela performs the following steps to deploy an inbound change:

1. She logs in to her sandbox org by typing https://login.
   salesforce.com.

2. She navigates to Setup (gear icon) ➤ Setup Home ➤ PLATFORM
   TOOLS ➤ Environments ➤ Change Sets ➤ Inbound Change Sets.

3. Then she navigates to the Change Sets Awaiting Deployment
   section, as shown in Figure 7-11. There she sees a list of inbound
   change sets (from sandboxes) that are awaiting deployment.

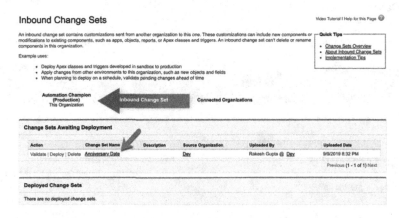

Figure 7-11. *Change sets awaiting deployment*

4. Pamela clicks the `Anniversary Date` inbound change set to view its details.

5. In the change sed Detail page, she notices two buttons: `Validate` and `Deploy`.

   - **Validate**: Pamela knows she can use this button to simulate an actual deployment. She would be able to view the success or failure messages received with an actual deployment.

   - **Deploy**: Pamela also knows that she uses the `Deploy` button to deploy the change set, which is done in a single operation. If the deployment is unable to complete (if it fails for any reason), the entire transaction is rolled back.

   Pamela knows the best practice is to validate the change set first. When it's successful, she would then deploy it.

6. Pamela clicks `Validate` and notes that the simulated change set deployment is a success.

7. She then deploys the change set by clicking `Deploy`. Pamela could select a test class to run, but she defaults and clicks `Deploy`. A warning message is shown that states that once a change set is deployed, it cannot be roll backed.

8. Pamela clicks the `OK` button and sees a message while the upload is in progress, as shown in Figure 7-12.

Change Set Detail
Anniversary Date
« Back to List: Inbound Change Sets

Video Tutorial | Help for this Page

This change set contains customizations that have been uploaded from a connected organization. If you aren't ready to deploy at this time, you can click Validate to preview deployment results without committing any changes. It isn't necessary to validate before deploying, as the deployment won't commit any changes if there are failures.

ℹ **Deployment Started**
Track the progress on the Deployment Status page

View Details   Validate Deploy Delete

Change Set Name	Anniversary Date	Source Organization	Dev
Description		Uploaded By	Rakesh Gupta, 9/9/2019 8:32 PM
Expiration Date	3/6/2020		

Figure 7-12. *Upload started*

9. When the upload is finished, whether a success or a failure,
    Pamela sees it listed in the Deployment History section, as shown
    in Figure 7-13.

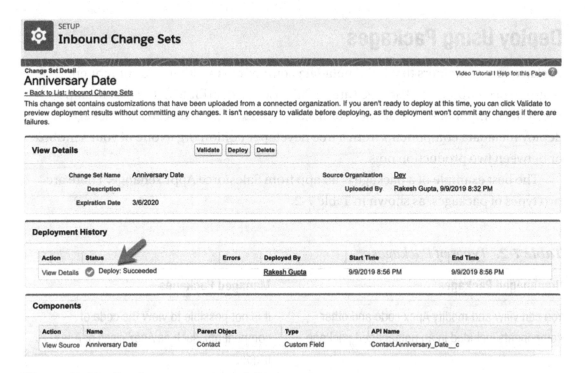

Figure 7-13. *Deployment successful*

If the status of the change set is Deploy: Succeeded, the change set was deployed
successfully.

Benefits of Using Change Sets

There are numerous advantages to using change sets for deployment:

1. There is a nice and tidy user interface to select changes that need
    to be deployed.

2. Change sets can be validated before deployment.

3. There is no need to install any other app to use change sets.

4. It is easy to clone a change set.

5. You can upload the same outbound change sets to multiple sandboxes or directly to a production org.

6. Change set deployment is tracked with an audit trail!

Deploy Using Packages

Packages are containers that hold metadata components—either one component or group of components. Packages are mainly used to distribute to the org the app's metadata components that are not connected. For example, you can use packages to deploy metadata components from a free developer edition org to one of your sandboxes or between two production orgs.

The best example of a package is an app from Salesforce AppExchange. There are two types of packages, as shown in Table 7-2.

Table 7-2. *Types of Packages*

Unmanaged Packages	Managed Packages
You can view and modify Apex code and other components included in an unmanaged package.	It is not possible to view the code of components, such as Apex class or Apex trigger.
Components can be edited in the organization after installation.	Components cannot be edited in the organization after installation.
The source organization has no control over the package after it is installed in a customer's org. Indeed, code within the package can be altered.	The code can only be altered in the source organization, where the package components were developed.
Unmanaged packages are generally used for module distribution among developers or freelancers.	Managed packages are generally used by Salesforce AppExchange partners to distribute apps to their customers.

The third type of package is called *unpackaged.* It refers to the components that exist natively in your organization, such as standard objects. Standard objects can go in an unpackaged package.

Points to Remember

1. E-mail deliverability for new and refreshed sandboxes must be set to system e-mail only.

2. You can create and manage sandboxes from the production org.

3. In a full sandbox, record IDs are identical to the production org's.

4. You can't use change sets to delete or rename components.

5. When deploying using a change set, the system runs all tests of Apex code. If your overall coverage is less than 75%, you will not be able to deploy a change set.

6. Change set deployment is tracked by an audit trail, which means you can check which components were deployed and when.

7. Use packages when you want to distribute your metadata components to customers across the globe.

8. To deploy metadata components through any tools requires system administrator permission.

Hands-on Exercises

The following exercises will give you more practice with the platform, which ultimately will help you in gaining mastery of it, and also will assist you in preparing for the certification examination. Remember, these are hands-on exercises, and you can find the answers at the back of the book in the Appendix, but try to implement them in your Salesforce org, which is the primary goal of doing them. But, try to do the exercises without looking at the answers!

1. True or False? It is possible to modify a trigger directly in a production org.

    a. True

    b. False

2. Which deployment tool activity is tracked by an audit trail?

    a. Change set

    b. Force.com IDE

    c. Package

    d. Force.com Workbench

3. Dennis Williams, a system administrator at GoC, created an
    application in his free developer org. Now he wants to share the
    application with his peers so they can use the application without
    seeing any code, and can provide their feedback. Which of the
    following deployment strategies Dennis should use?

    a. Change sets

    b. Managed packages

    c. Unmanaged packages

    d. SFDX

4. Dennis Williams receives a requirement to create a sandbox that
    brings all Lead records from production. GoC has 25,000 leads at
    the moment. Which sandbox should Dennis use?

    a. Developer

    b. Developer pro

    c. Partial copy

    d. Full

5. Dennis Williams receives a requirement to create a sandbox for
    regression testing. GoC just completed an integration with one
    of the leading banks in the United States and is planning to start
    integration testing, which may create millions of record. Which of
    the following sandboxes should Dennis use?

a. Developer

b. Developer pro

c. Partial copy

d. Full

Summary

In this chapter, we looked at the limits of declarative development vs. programmatic development. We also went through the application development life cycle. Furthermore, we studied different sandbox types. Last, we examined the deployment process in Salesforce by using an example. In Chapter 8, we take a look at the social and reporting capabilities of the Salesforce platform.

CHAPTER 8

The Power of Social Analytics

In Chapter 7, we covered limits of declarative customization and studied when to use programmatic development. We then explored various types of sandboxes. Last, we discussed different deployment tools in Salesforce using a few real-life examples.

This chapter is comprised of three parts. In part one, we walk through the capabilities of social features through some use cases. In part two, we take a look at reports and report types. In part three, we examine the role dashboards play in rendering underlying analytics.

Social Features

Salesforce social features allow users to connect accounts, contacts, and leads to social networks such as Twitter and YouTube. By so doing, users can keep abreast of the latest activities in their organization's accounts, contacts, and leads in the social ecosystem. In the Winter'20 release of Salesforce, only Twitter will be available in Lightning Experience; in Classic, however, both Twitter and YouTube are accessible.

By default, social features for accounts, contacts, and leads are enabled in all orgs.

Update Social Accounts, Contacts, and Leads Settings

Now that you understand what social features Salesforce offers, it is time see how to update the settings for social accounts in an org. Let's join Pamela Kline once again. Her manager has requested that she make sure GoC users are not able to access information about their accounts, contacts, and leads using YouTube.

211

© Rakesh Gupta 2020
R. Gupta, *Salesforce Platform App Builder Certification*, https://doi.org/10.1007/978-1-4842-5479-0_8

Pamela meets her manager's requirement by performing the following steps:

1. She navigates to Setup (gear icon) ➤ Setup ➤ Feature Settings
   ➤ Sales ➤ Social Accounts and Contacts Settings.

2. Next, Pamela deselects the Enable YouTube check box, as shown
   in Figure 8-1.

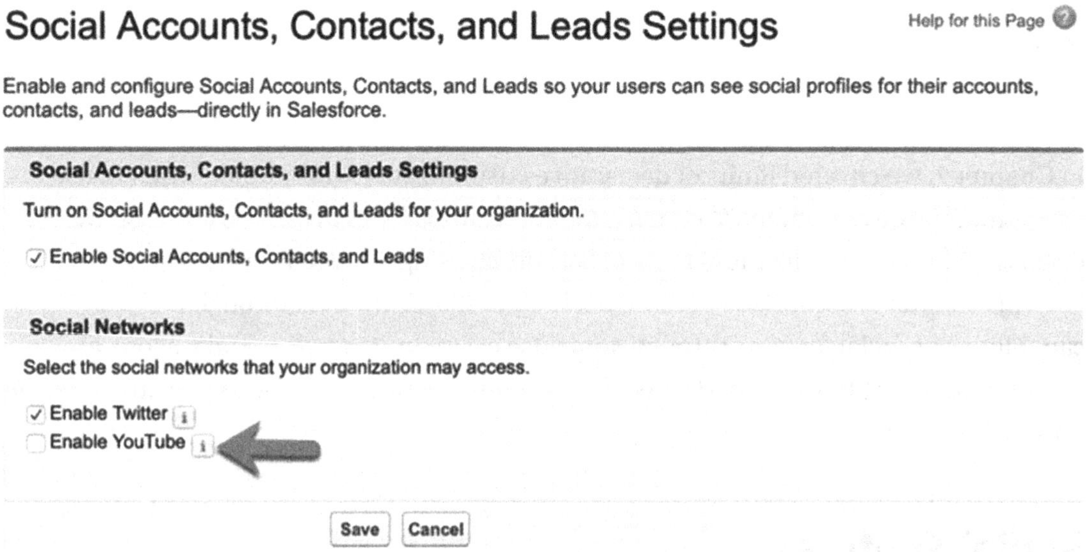

Figure 8-1. Social Accounts, Contacts, and Lead Settings section

3. When done, she clicks the Save button.

Going forward, GoC users will only be able to access Twitter by default. Pamela immediately informs GoC users of this change and notes they may configure Social Accounts, Contacts, and Leads for their individual use.

Hide Social Network Profiles

If Social Accounts, Contacts, and Leads is enabled in your org, and some users do not want to use it, they can hide it by navigating to their personal settings.

Richard Adams is working as a senior sales director at GoC. He does not want to use Social Accounts, Contacts, and Leads features. Let's help hide these features.

Tell Richard to follow the steps listed here to hide the Social Accounts, Contacts, and Leads features:

1. Navigate to Personal Settings ➤ Display & Layout ➤ My Social Accounts and Contacts.

2. Uncheck the Use Social Accounts and Contacts check box, as shown in Figure 8-2.

My Social Accounts and Contacts Settings

See social profiles for your accounts, contacts, leads, and person accounts—directly in Salesforce.

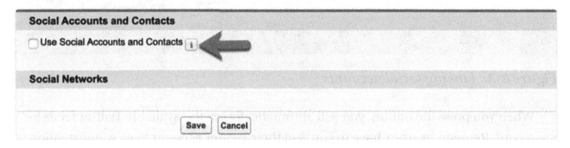

Figure 8-2. *My Social Accounts and Contacts Settings section*

3. Click the Save button.

Link Twitter Profiles to Accounts, Contacts, and Leads

To connect an account with Twitter, go to that account and sign in to Twitter using your credentials. In Lightning Experience, find the Sign in with Twitter button on the record's News tab, as shown in Figure 8-3.

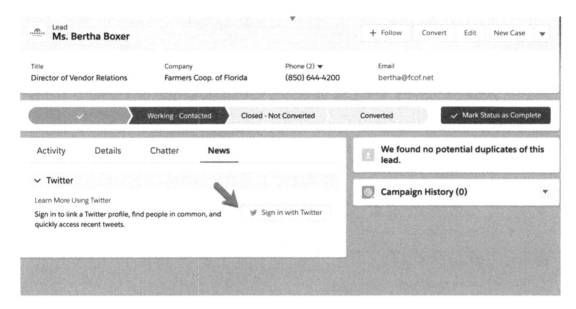

Figure 8-3. *Linking social accounts*

When you press the button, you will automatically see the available Twitter feeds for the record. Remember, users have to connect their Twitter account to view information from an account's Twitter feed. Salesforce doesn't store any Twitter data; all you see is a-real time feed fetched by Salesforce.

Introduction to Reports

Reports are a way to analyze how efficient teams are performing over time. For example, GoC's senior sales director, Richard Adams, wants to know the effectiveness of a campaign that ran during the current fiscal year. The campaign's report showed the current status of leads that came via referral.

Reports always generate data in real time based on the criteria you define. Reports respect an organization's security and settings. As a result, users only see records in the reports to which they have access.

To share reports with users, save them in a folder. Then, share folder access with the users. It is possible to create reports for standard and custom objects.

When you create reports in Salesforce, you must select a report type. A report type is nothing but a holding tank for records from one or multiple objects.

Report Types

Report types come in two flavors:

1. Standard report types

2. Custom report types

Standard Report Type

By default, standard report types are available for building reports on standard and custom objects, and *their* related objects. When a system administrator creates a new custom field, the field is automatically added to standard report types.

Custom Report Type

A custom report type allows you to build your own data set or container. Users can select a report type in the report wizard to create a report. Remember the following key concepts when creating custom report types:

- You are allowed to select combinations of up to four related objects.

- You can select an object's fields (parent to child) and use them as columns in a report.

Setting up a Custom Report Type

Salesforce provides a simple wizard to create custom report types. Let's rejoin Pamela. She has received a requirement from her manager to create a report that lists all accounts that have at least one contact record, and each contact record must have at least one related opportunity associated with it. Pamela performs the following steps to create a custom report type for the preceding business requirement:

1. She navigates to Setup (gear icon) ➤ Setup Home ➤ Feature Settings ➤ Analytics ➤ Report & Dashboards ➤ Report Types.

2. She clicks the New Custom Report Types button, which opens a window where she enters the following details:

   - **Primary Object**: Pamela selects the primary object from all the objects available in her organization, even those she doesn't have permission to view! In this case, Pamela selects the Account object.

- **Report Type Label**: She enters a meaningful name for the report type label: `Accounts with Contact and Opportunity`.

- **Report Type Name**: This field is autopopulated based on the report type label.

- **Description**: Pamela writes some meaningful text so other developers and administrators can understand easily why this custom report type was created in the first place.

- **Store in Category**: She select the `Account & Contacts` category to store her custom report type.

- **Deployment Status**: Pamela selects `Deployed.` Her screen looks like Figure 8-4.

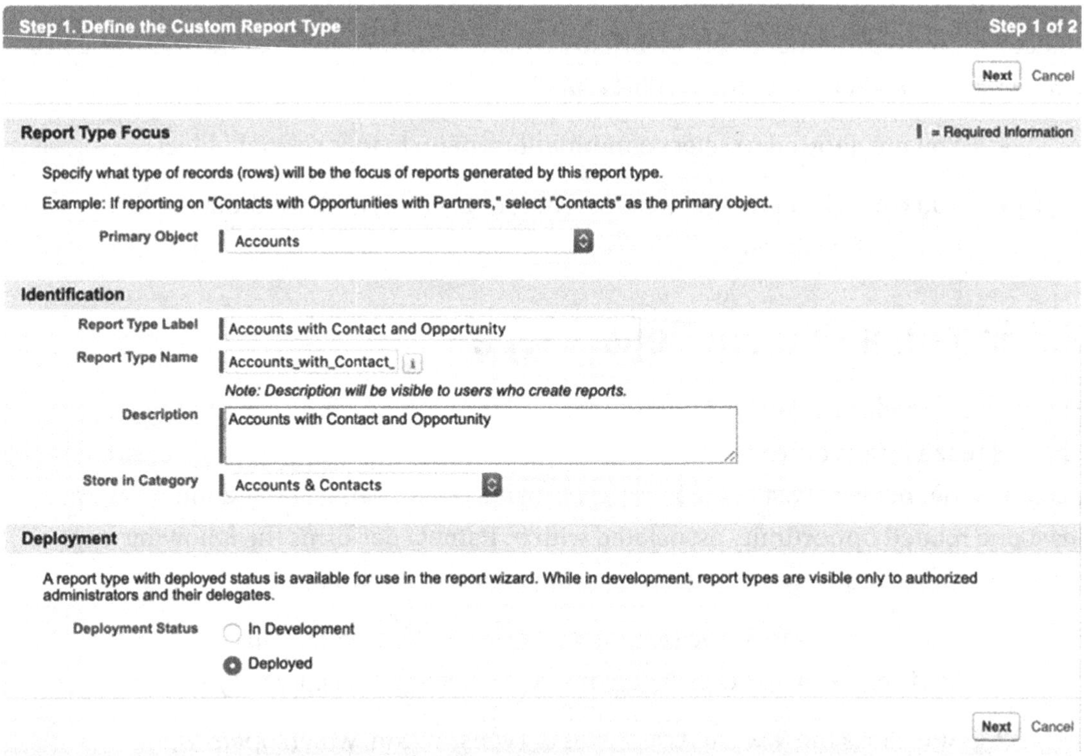

Step 1. Define the Custom Report Type	Step 1 of 2

Next   Cancel

Report Type Focus   ❚ = Required Information

Specify what type of records (rows) will be the focus of reports generated by this report type.

Example: If reporting on "Contacts with Opportunities with Partners," select "Contacts" as the primary object.

Primary Object | Accounts |

Identification

Report Type Label | Accounts with Contact and Opportunity |

Report Type Name | Accounts_with_Contact_ | i

Note: Description will be visible to users who create reports.

Description | Accounts with Contact and Opportunity |

Store in Category | Accounts & Contacts |

Deployment

A report type with deployed status is available for use in the report wizard. While in development, report types are visible only to authorized administrators and their delegates.

Deployment Status   ○ In Development
                     ● Deployed

Next   Cancel

Figure 8-4. *Defining the custom report type*

3. When done, Pamela clicks the Next button.

4. With Account as her primary object, she now needs to relate another object to it. She selects Contacts as her secondary object and then selects the check box Each "A" record must have at least one related "B" record. She then selects Opportunities as the tertiary object and selects the check box Each "B" record must have at least one related "C" record, as shown in Figure 8-5.

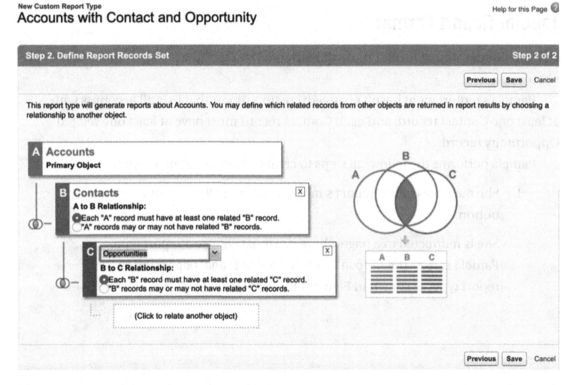

Figure 8-5. *Defining the report records set*

5. When done, Pamela clicks the Save button.

Report Format Types

Salesforce allows you to generate reports and assign them a format based on your business requirement. Salesforce has four different report formats:

1. Tabular

2. Summary

3. Matrix

4. Joined

Tabular Report Format

Use the tabular report format to display rows of records in a table without any subtotal.

Pamela's requirement hasn't changed: create a report that lists all accounts with at least one Contact record, and each Contact record must have at least one related Opportunity record.

Pamela performs the following steps to create a custom tabular report:

1. She navigates to the Reports tab and clicks the New Report button.

2. She is redirected to a page where she must choose a report type. Pamela selects the Accounts with Contact and Opportunity report type, as shown in Figure 8-6.

Choose Report Type

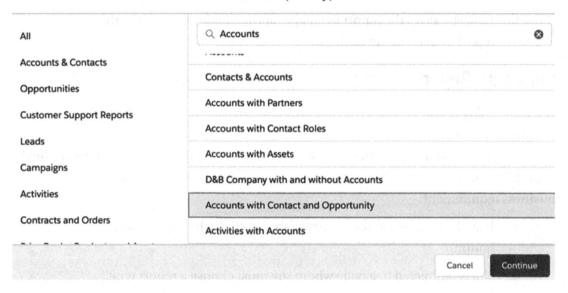

Figure 8-6. *Choosing a report type*

3. When done, she clicks the Continue button.

4. In the next screen, she adjusts the filter by changing the Date field filter by selecting Created Date with the range All Time (Figure 8-7).

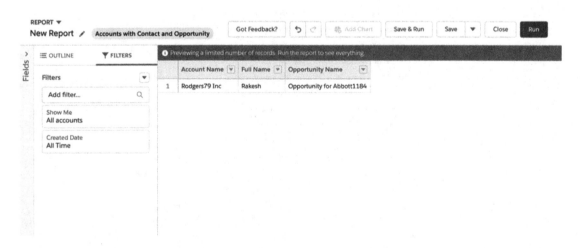

Figure 8-7. *Custom report*

5. When done, she clicks the Save button.

6. Last, she saves the report to an appropriate folder and checks the report folder sharing settings.

Summary Report Format

Use a summary report format to display groupings of rows of data. Let's start with a business use case.

Pamela receives a requirement to create a summary report that groups leads by lead source. She performs the following steps to create a custom report for the preceding business requirement:

1. Pamela navigates to the Reports tab and clicks the New Report button.

2. She is redirected to a page where she must choose a report type. Pamela selects the Leads report type.

3. To apply row grouping based on lead source, she clicks the Lead Source drop-down, then Group Rows by This Field, as shown in Figure 8-8 (numbers 1 and 2, respectively).

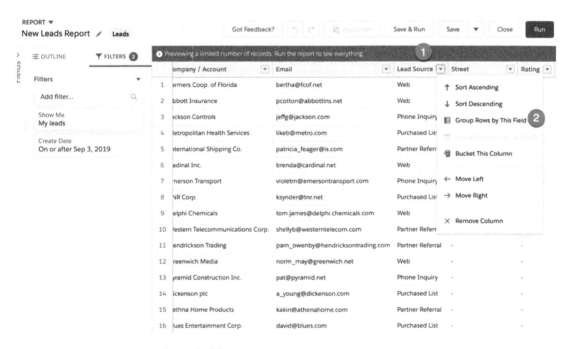

Figure 8-8. *Grouping by a field*

4. When done, she clicks the Save button.

5. She names the report "Leads grouped by source" and saves it in the Unfiled Public Reports folder.

6. When done, she clicks the Save button.

Matrix Report Format

The matrix report is the most complex report format. Use this report to summarize data in a grid. You can group records by both columns and rows. Let us start with a business use case.

Previously, Pamela created the report "Leads grouped by source." She receives another requirement to display on the report who owns these Lead records. Pamela performs the following steps to create a matrix report for the preceding business requirement:

1. Pamela navigates to the Reports tab and clicks Leads grouped by source, then she clicks the Edit button.

2. She then applies column grouping based on the lead owner by clicking the drop-down Lead Owner and selecting Group Columns by This Field, as shown in Figure 8-9 (numbers 1 and 2, respectively).

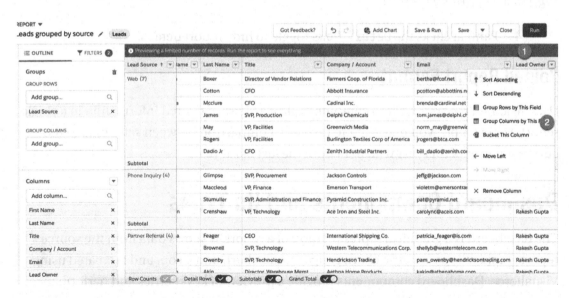

Figure 8-9. *Grouping by a field*

3. When done, she clicks the Save button.

Now the report automatically changes the format from summary to matrix (Figure 8-10).

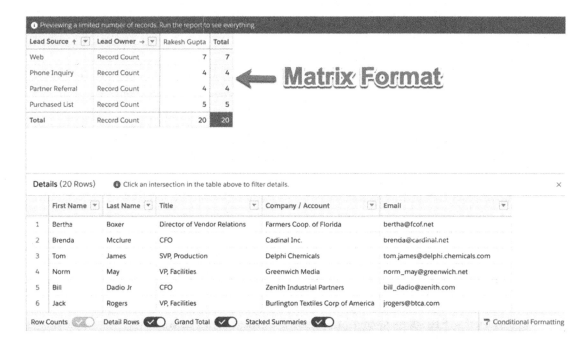

Figure 8-10. Matrix report

4. Pamela clicks the Detail Rows toggle to hide report details.

Joined Report Format

Use the joined report format to combine multiple views of related information in a single report. For example, you may want to display a comparison between sales data in the current quarter of this year with data from the last fiscal year.

Dashboard Components and Its Types

The dashboard is a graphical representation of a report. It shows data from the source report graphically as a metric chart, gauge, donut chart, and so on, and is created using Visualforce. Dashboard components provide a preview of key metrics and performance meters of your organization.

Business users can see all the details on a dashboard, regardless of the type of access they have to the records. But, as soon as they drill down to reports, users only see the records to which they have access.

Creating a Dashboard

A dynamic dashboard displays data on the dashboard based on the logged-in user. Dashboards can be created from summary and matrix reports only. When using Lightning Experience, you can even use a joined report as a source for a dashboard. You can also use a tabular report as a source if you put a limit on the number of rows it returns. Let's revisit Pamela.

If you recall, Pamela created the matrix report "Leads grouped by source." Now she wants to create a dynamic dashboard for it. She performs the following steps to do so:

1. Pamela navigates to the Dashboards tab and clicks the New Dashboard button.

2. She is redirected to a page where she has to enter the dashboard name. In this case, Pamela types Lead Dashboard and selects a folder to store the dashboard. She then clicks Create, as shown in Figure 8-11.

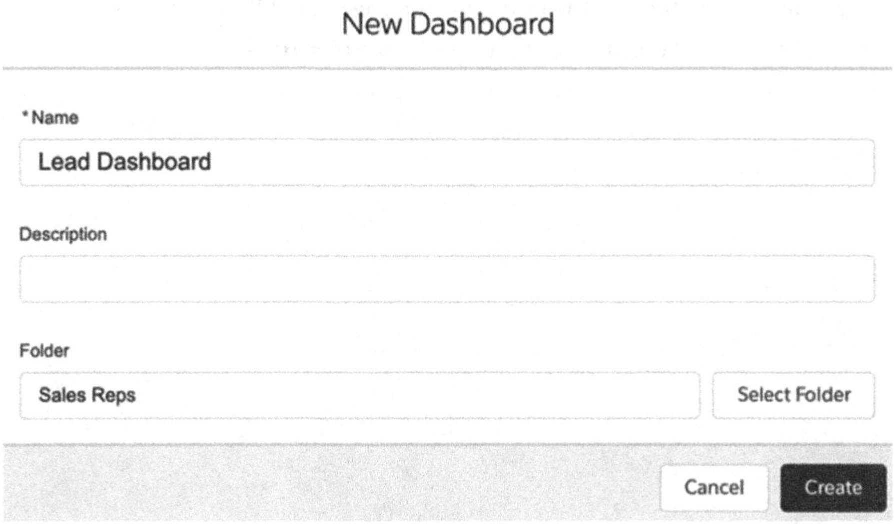

Figure 8-11. *Creating a new dashboard*

3. Next, Pamela clicks + Component to insert a component onto the dashboard.

4. She receives a prompt to select the report, so she selects Leads group by source, as shown in Figure 8-12.

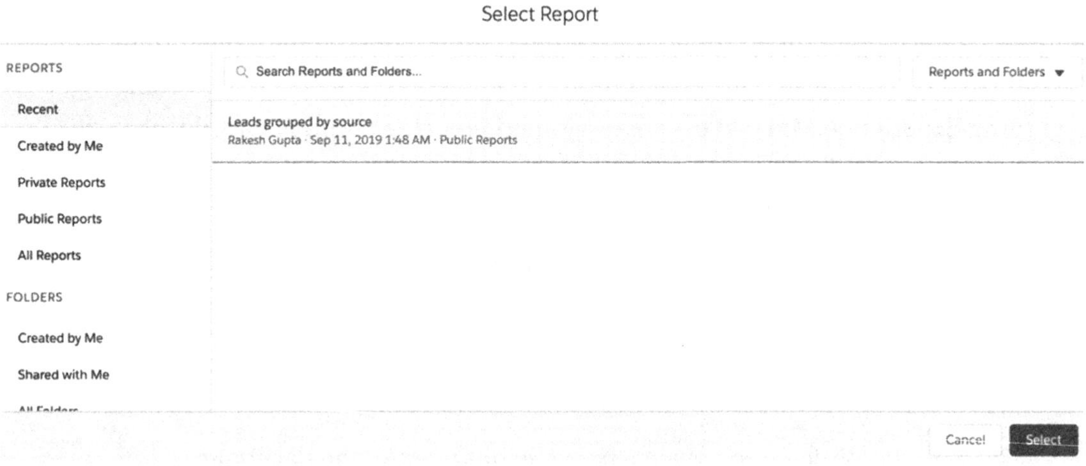

Select Report

REPORTS	Q Search Reports and Folders...	Reports and Folders ▼
Recent		
Created by Me	Leads grouped by source Rakesh Gupta · Sep 11, 2019 1:48 AM · Public Reports	
Private Reports		
Public Reports		
All Reports		
FOLDERS		
Created by Me		
Shared with Me		
All Folders		

Cancel   Select

Figure 8-12. *Selecting a report*

5. When done, she clicks the Select button.

6. Next, she adds the component—in this case, she clicks the funnel chart icon—and configures it, as shown in Figure 8-13.

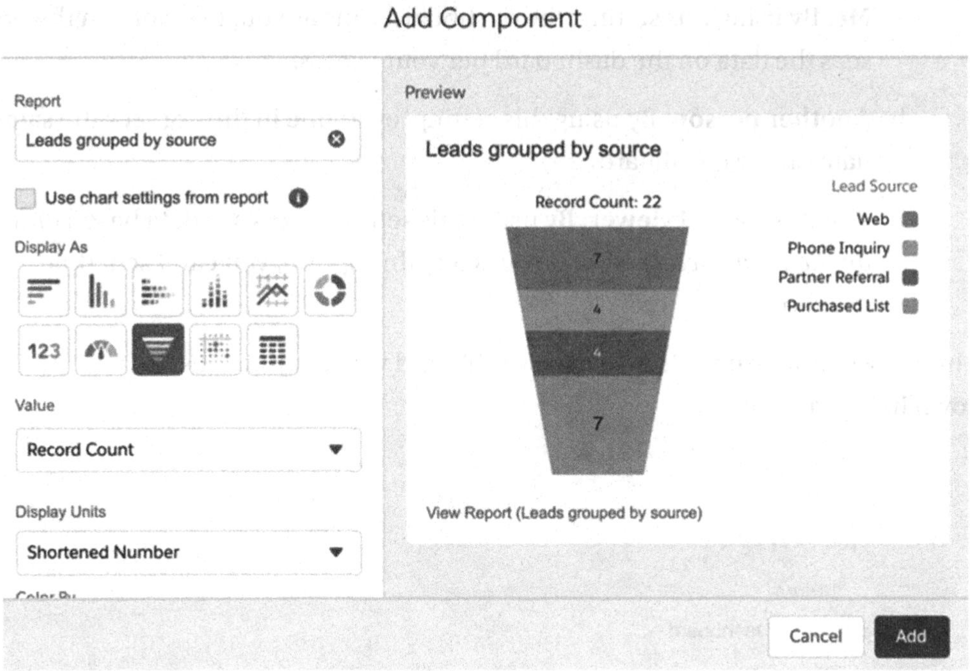

Add Component

Report

Leads grouped by source   ⊗

☐ Use chart settings from report   ⓘ

Display As

Value

Record Count   ▼

Display Units

Shortened Number   ▼

Color By

Preview

Leads grouped by source

Record Count: 22

Lead Source

Web ▪
Phone Inquiry ▪
Partner Referral ▪
Purchased List ▪

7

4

4

7

View Report (Leads grouped by source)

Cancel   Add

Figure 8-13. *Adding a component*

7. She can add multiple components to her dashboard. Each component shows data from one report. Pamela adds one more component—a donut chart—to her dashboard. She uses the drag-and-drop feature to reposition her components.

8. When done, she clicks the Save button.

Making a Dashboard Dynamic

To make her dashboard dynamic, Pamela must go back to the dashboard she just created and perform the following steps.

1. She navigates to the Dashboard tab and opens Lead Dashboard.

2. She clicks the Edit button.

3. Next, she clicks Properties and goes to the View Dashboard As section. There are three possible options provided by Salesforce:

a. **Me**: By using this setting, the dashboard runs as you. Everyone in the org sees the data on the dashboard per your access.

b. **Another person**: By using this setting, everyone in the org sees the same data on the dashboard.

c. **The dashboard viewer**: By using this setting, users see data based *only on their own access level*. If you select this option, you can't schedule dashboard.

In this scenario, Pamela selects The dashboard viewer option, as shown in Figure 8-14.

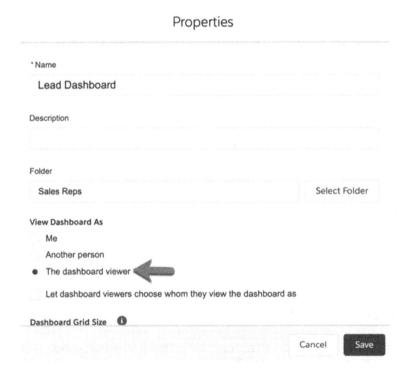

Properties

*Name

Lead Dashboard

Description

Folder

Sales Reps   Select Folder

View Dashboard As

Me

Another person

● The dashboard viewer

Let dashboard viewers choose whom they view the dashboard as

Dashboard Grid Size ⓘ

Cancel   Save

Figure 8-14. *Viewing the dashboard as*

4. When done, she clicks the Save button.

Points to Remember

1. Your accounts, contacts, and leads aren't notified when you use Salesforce to view their social network profiles.

2. Salesforce doesn't import, or store, your social information. Each time you select a social profile or a YouTube video, Salesforce retrieves the information you want to see directly from the social network in real time.

3. System administrators or users who have Run Reports and Manage Dashboards permission can create dashboards.

4. If you can't see the Add Formula option in the Fields section of the report builder, change your report format to summary, matrix, or joined. Formulas don't show up for tabular reports.

5. You can have 20 filter fields and up to five formula fields per report.

6. By default, reports timeout after ten minutes. You can contact Salesforce.com support to extend the timeout limit to 20 minutes for tabular, summary, and matrix reports. But, note that an extension of the timeout limit is not available for joined reports. Joined reports continue to timeout every ten minutes.

7. The maximum number of source report columns you can map to target fields is 100.

Hands-on Exercises

The following exercises will give you more practice with the platform, which ultimately will help you in gaining mastery of it, and also will assist you in preparing for the certification examination. Remember, these are hands-on exercises, and you can find the answers at the back of the book in the Appendix, but try to implement them in your Salesforce org, which is the primary goal of doing them. But, try to do the exercises without looking at the answers!

1. What are the components of the dashboard that use grand totals? Select two options.

   a. Metric

   b. Table

   c. Gauge

   d. Chart

2. Which report type is used to group rows of data and show their subtotals?

   a. Summary

   b. Matrix

   c. Tabular

   d. Detailed

3. Which report type is used to group rows and columns of data and show their subtotals?

   a. Summary

   b. Matrix

   c. Tabular

   d. Detailed

4. Dennis Williams, a system administrator at GoC, has received a requirement to create a report that shows leads created from social media as a source, their current stage, and who owns the lead. How would you instruct Dennis to meet this requirement?

5. Dennis Williams receives a requirement to show opportunities from the last, and current, fiscal year by opportunity owner. How would you instruct Dennis to meet this requirement?

Summary

In this chapter, we discussed the social features of Salesforce for accounts, contacts, and leads. We also went through the reporting concepts in Salesforce, including custom report types and different report formats. Last, we examined the dashboard and dynamic dashboard concepts.

After reading this book, you should have gained a good understanding of Salesforce fundamentals and, as a result, should feel confident enough to take the Platform App Builder certification exam. Before you take the exam, make sure to complete this Trailmix on Trailhead: `https://trailhead.salesforce.com/users/strailhead/ trailmixes/prepare-for-your-salesforce-platform-app-builder-credential`. Good luck!

Answers to Hands-on Exercises

Chapter 1

1. b
2. b
3. c

Chapter 2

1. This is an exercise to explore the database architecture. There is no answer.

2. Use the Date field type. Refer to Chapter 2 to learn how to set up field-level security using Schema Builder.

3. Dennis should use the field types Text (Encrypted) and Mask All Characters.

4. Dennis should use the field type Text Area (Rich).

5. Dennis should use the field type Geolocation.

6. Dennis should select the field type Formula field. It will be resolved by the Formula field because this field is dynamic and always displays the current site value from the parent account.

7. This is a straightforward exercise. There is no "correct" answer.

© Rakesh Gupta 2020
R. Gupta, *Salesforce Platform App Builder Certification*, https://doi.org/10.1007/978-1-4842-5479-0

8. Dennis should use the field type `Master Detail Relationship`.

9. Advise Dennis to do the following:

    a. Select field type `Lookup Relationship`.

    b. Select the following options, while creating the `Lookup Relationship` field:

        •   Always require a value in this field in order to save a record.

        •   For `What to do if the lookup record is deleted?` select `Don't allow deletion of the lookup record that's part of a lookup relationship`.

10. This is a straightforward exercise. There is no "correct" answer.

11. This is a straightforward exercise. There is no "correct" answer.

Chapter 3

1. b

2. Set object OWD to Private; `Grant Access Using Hierarchies` = False.

3.

    a. Set OWD = Private; create a public group that includes the roles CEO, COO, Sales Rep-EMEA, Sales Rep-AMER, and the two users the from Sales Rep-APAC profile. Then, create sharing to grant Read Only access to the public group.

    b. Update the record owner to Pamela and make sure she has a role assigned.

    c. Via profile only, grant Read access on the `Address__c` object to all profiles.

4. Create a field `Social Security Number` with data type `Text (Encrypted)`, create a permission set to grant View Encrypted Data permission, and assign this permission set to the users mentioned.

5. c, because there are just ten records. We don't want to share all records owned by VP Sales.

6. The system administrator doesn't have a role assigned. If the system administrator—in this case, Dennis—has a role assigned, then he is below the CEO in the role hierarchy. Also, Dennis doesn't have Delete permission on the `Address__c` object.

7. The system administrator doesn't have a role assigned. If the system administrator—in this case, Dennis—has a role assigned, then he is below the CEO in the role hierarchy. Also, Dennis doesn't have Edit permission on the `Address__c` object.

8. Use Apex-managed sharing.

9. Set the Sales Rep-AMER profile `Lead` object access to Read, use a permission set and add Assign permission to it, and assign the permission set to the three Sales Rep-AMER users.

10. Use a permission set to add View All permission for the `Lead` object.

11. Use criteria-based sharing.

12. Set Lead OWD to Private, create a public group with all users except Rakesh and Munira, then write a sharing rule to grant Read access to the public group.

13. Set `Contact` OWD to be controlled by the parent.

14. Use Apex-managed sharing.

Chapter 4

1. This is straightforward.

2. Use a custom button or link.

3. Tell him to use component visibility features.

4. Tell him to use a quick action to update `Lead  Status`.

5. This is straightforward. Include your findings about the Lightning app logo.

Chapter 5

1. Use lead support processes and record types.

2. Customize the Lead Lightning page and add its respective components.

3. Use lookup filters.

4. Use lookup filters.

5. Add a custom field.

6. Use lookup filters.

7.

    a. Use a validation rule.

    b. Use a custom permission in the validation rule and then assign it to users or profiles.

8. Use a formula field.

9. Use validation rules.

10. Use a rollup summary field.

Chapter 6

1. You have to use the Screen element to take the user input and display the outcome. But, to calculate the sum, you may have to use a formula.

2. Tell him to use an e-mail alert and Process Builder's immediate action Send Email.

3. Tell him to use Process Builder's immediate action Update Records to update the contact phone number.

4.

    a. Use the `Post to Chatter` action in Process Builder.

    b. Use the `Update Records` action in Process Builder.

    c. Use the `Send Custom Notification` action in Process Builder.

5. Tell him to use the Lightning Flow `Create Records` element and Process Builder to launch the flow.

Chapter 7

1. b

2. a

3. b

4. c

5. d

Chapter 8

1. a and c

2. a

3. b

4. Use a matrix report in which rows are grouped by stage and columns are grouped by owner.

5. Create a Summary report, with filter last and current fiscal year. Apply group by opportunity owner.

Index

A

Account object, 5
Apex-managed sharing, 79
Apex programming skills, 146
AppExchange, benefits, 18, 19
App Launcher, 95
Application life cycle management
    development stage, 193
    governance, 192
    operations, 193
Approval process, Salesforce
    activation, 186
    automated process, 176
    creation, wizards, 176
    detail page, 182
    entry specification, 177
    final approval action, 182, 183
    initial submission action, 183, 184
    lightning experience, 176
    Record editability properties
        field, 178
    request page, 180
    specifying initial submitters, 181
    steps, 184, 186
Artificial intelligence (AI), 12
Automate business processes, 148

B

Business requirement, 159

C

CEO's role hierarchy, 65, 66
Chief operating officer (COO), 63
Computer telephony integration (CTI), 10
Cross-object formula, 125
Customer relationship management
    (CRM), 1
Custom fields, creation, 29, 30
Custom objects, 6
Custom report type
    business requirement, 215, 216
    creation, 215
    defining, 216, 217

D

Dashboard components
    creation, 223–225
    graphical representation, 222
    viewing, 225, 226
Data Model, 27, 28
Declarative development
    Apex trigger, 190
    APIs use, 192
    AppExchange apps, 191
    limitations, 190
    visualforce page, 190
Deployment
    change sets, 198
        benefits, 205

237